SILVER EDITION

Teacher's Edition with Tests

Interactions 1

WRITING

Cheryl Pavlik

Margaret Keenan Segal

Teacher's Edition by Edward J. Scarry

McGraw Hill

Interactions 1 Writing Teacher's Edition with Tests, Silver Edition

Published by McGraw-Hill ESL/ELT, a business unit of The McGraw-Hill Companies, Inc. 1221 Avenue of the Americas, New York, NY 10020. Copyright © 2007 by The McGraw-Hill Companies, Inc. All rights reserved. No part of this publication may be reproduced or distributed in any form or by any means, or stored in a database or retrieval system, without the prior written consent of The McGraw-Hill Companies, Inc., including, but not limited to, in any network or other electronic storage or transmission, or broadcast for distance learning.

ISBN 13: 978-0-07-328392-0 (Teacher's Edition)
ISBN 10: 0-07-328392-4
2 3 4 5 6 7 8 9 10 EUS 11 10 09 08 07

Editorial director: Erik Gundersen
Series editor: Valerie Kelemen
Developmental editors: Janet Gokay, Jennifer Wilson Cooper
Production manager: Juanita Thompson
Production coordinator: James D. Gwyn
Cover designer: Robin Locke Monda
Interior designer: Nesbitt Graphics, Inc.

Cover photo: Steve Allen/Creatas Images

www.esl-elt.mcgraw-hill.com

The **McGraw·Hill** Companies

Table of Contents

Introduction

Student Book Teaching Notes and Answer Keys

Welcome to the Teacher's Edition

The Teacher's Edition of *Interactions/Mosaic* Silver Edition provides support and flexibility to teachers using the *Interactions/Mosaic* Silver Edition 18-book academic skills series. The Teacher's Edition provides step-by-step guidance for implementing each activity in the Student Book. The Teacher's Edition also provides expansion activities with photocopiable masters of select expansion activities, identification of activities that support a Best Practice, valuable notes on content, answer keys, audioscripts, end-of-chapter tests, and placement tests. Each chapter in the Teacher's Edition begins with an overview of the content, vocabulary, and teaching goals in that chapter. Each chapter in the Student Book begins with an engaging photo and related discussion questions that strengthen the educational experience and connect students to the topic.

■ Procedural Notes

The procedural notes are useful for both experienced and new teachers. Experienced teachers can use the bulleted, step-by step procedural notes as a quick guide and refresher before class, while newer or substitute teachers can use the notes as a more extensive guide to assist them in the classroom. The procedural notes guide teachers through each strategy and activity; describe what materials teachers might need for an activity; and help teachers provide context for the activities.

■ Answer Keys

Answer keys are provided for all activities that have definite answers. For items that have multiple correct answers, various possible answers are provided. The answer key follows the procedural note for the relevant activity. Answer keys are also provided for the Chapter Tests and the Placement Tests.

■ Expansion Activities

A number of expansion activities with procedural notes are included in each chapter. These activities offer teachers creative ideas for reinforcing the chapter content while appealing to different learning styles. Activities include games, conversation practice, presentations, and projects. These expansion activities often allow students to practice integrated language skills, not just the skills that the student book focuses on. Some of the expansion activities include photocopiable black line masters included in the back of the book.

■ Content Notes

Where appropriate, content notes are included in the Teacher's Edition. These are notes that might illuminate or enhance a learning point in the activity and might help teachers answer student questions about the content. These notes are provided at the logical point of use, but teachers can decide if and when to use the information in class.

■ Chapter Tests

Each chapter includes a chapter test that was designed to test the vocabulary, reading, writing, grammar, and/or listening strategies taught in the chapter, depending on the language skill strand being used. Teachers can simply copy and distribute the tests, then use the answer keys found in the Teacher's Edition. The purpose of the chapter tests is not only to assess students' understanding of material covered in the chapter but also to give students an idea of how they are doing and what they need to work on. Each chapter test has four parts with items totaling 100 points. Item types include multiple choice, fill-in-the blank, and true/false. Audioscripts are provided when used.

■ Black Line Masters (Photocopiable Masters)

Each chapter includes a number of expansion activities with black line masters, or master worksheets, that teachers can copy and distribute. These activities and black line masters are optional. They can help reinforce and expand on chapter material in an engaging way. Activities include games;

conversation practice; working with manipulatives such as sentence strips; projects; and presentations. Procedural notes and answer keys (when applicable) are provided in the Teacher's Edition.

- **Placement Tests**

  Each of the four language skill strands has a placement test designed to help assess in which level the student belongs. Each test has been constructed to be given in under an hour. Be sure to go over the directions and answer any questions before the test begins. Students are instructed not to ask questions once the test begins. Following each placement test, you'll find a scoring placement key that suggests the appropriate book to be used based on the number of items answered correctly. Teachers should use judgment in placing students and selecting texts.

The Interactions/Mosaic Silver Edition Program

Interactions/Mosaic Silver Edition is a fully-integrated, 18-book academic skills series. Language proficiencies are articulated from the beginning through advance levels <u>within</u> each of the four language skill strands. Chapter themes articulate <u>across</u> the four skill strands to systematically recycle content, vocabulary, and grammar.

- **Reading Strand**

  Reading skills and strategies are strategically presented and practiced through a variety of themes and reading genres in the five Reading books. Pre-reading, reading, and post-reading activities include strategies and activities that aid comprehension, build vocabulary, and prepare students for academic success. Each chapter includes at least two readings that center around the same theme, allowing students to deepen their understanding of a topic and command of vocabulary related to that topic. Readings include magazine articles, textbook passages, essays, letters, and website articles. They explore, and guide the student to explore, stimulating topics. Vocabulary is presented before each reading and is built on throughout the chapter. High-frequency words and words from the Academic Word List are focused on and pointed out with asterisks (*) in each chapter's Self-Assessment Log.

- **Listening/Speaking Strand**

  A variety of listening input, including lectures, academic discussions, and conversations help students explore stimulating topics in the five Listening/Speaking books. Activities associated with the listening input, such as pre-listening tasks, systematically guide students through strategies and critical thinking skills that help prepare them for academic achievement. In the Interactions books, the activities are coupled with instructional photos featuring a cast of engaging, multi-ethnic students participating in North American college life. Across the strand, lectures and dialogues are broken down into manageable parts giving students an opportunity to predict, identify main ideas, and effectively manage lengthy input. Questions, guided discussion activities, and structured pair and group work stimulate interest and interaction among students, often culminating in organizing their information and ideas in a graphic organizer, writing, and/or making a presentation to the class. Pronunciation is highlighted in every chapter, an aid to improving both listening comprehension and speaking fluency. Enhanced focus on vocabulary building is developed throughout and a list of target words for each chapter is provided so students can interact meaningfully with the material. Finally, Online Learning Center features MP3 files from the Student Book audio program for students to download onto portable digital audio players.

- **Writing Strand**

  Activities in each of the four Writing books are systematically structured to culminate in a *Writing Product* task. Activities build on key elements of writing from sentence development to writing single paragraphs, articles, narratives, and essays of multiple lengths and genres. Connections between writing and grammar tie the writing skill in focus with the grammar structures needed to develop each writing skill. Academic themes, activities, writing topics, vocabulary development, and critical thinking strategies prepare students for university life. Instructional photos are used to strengthen engagement and the educational experience. Explicit pre-writing questions and discussions activate prior knowledge, help organize ideas and information, and create a foundation for the writing product. Each chapter includes a self-evaluation rubric which supports the learner as he or she builds confidence and autonomy in academic writing. Finally, the Writing Articulation Chart helps teachers see the progression of writing strategies both in terms of mechanics and writing genres.

■ **Grammar Strand**

Questions and topical quotes in the four Grammar books, coupled with instructional photos stimulate interest, activate prior knowledge, and launch the topic of each chapter. Engaging academic topics provide context for the grammar and stimulate interest in content as well as grammar. A variety of activity types, including individual, pair, and group work, allow students to build grammar skills and use the grammar they are learning in activities that cultivate critical thinking skills. Students can refer to grammar charts to review or learn the form and function of each grammar point. These charts are numbered sequentially, formatted consistently, and indexed systematically, providing lifelong reference value for students.

■ **Focus on Testing for the TOEFL® iBT**

The all-new TOEFL® iBT *Focus on Testing* sections prepare students for success on the TOEFL® iBT by presenting and practicing specific strategies for each language skill area. The Focus on Testing sections are introduced in Interactions 1 and are included in all subsequent levels of the Reading, Listening/Speaking, and Writing strands. These strategies focus on what The Educational Testing Service (ETS) has identified as the target skills in each language skill area. For example, "reading for basic comprehension" (identifying the main idea, understanding pronoun reference) is a target reading skill and is presented and practiced in one or more *Focus on Testing* sections. In addition, this and other target skills are presented and practiced in chapter components outside the *Focus on Testing* sections and have special relevance to the TOEFL® iBT. For example, note-taking is an important test-taking strategy, particularly in the listening section of the TOEFL® iBT, and is included in activities within each of the Listening/Speaking books. All but two of the *Interactions/Mosaic* titles have a *Focus on Testing* section. Although *Interactions Access Reading* and *Interaction Access Listening/Speaking* don't include these sections because of their level, they do present and develop skills that will prepare students for the TOEFL® iBT.

■ **Best Practices**

In each chapter of this Teacher's Edition, you'll find Best Practices boxes that highlight a particular activity and show how this activity is tied to a particular Best Practice. The Interactions/Mosaic Silver Edition team of writers, editors, and teacher consultants has identified the following six interconnected Best Practices.

---

* TOEFL is a registered trademark of Educational Testing Services (ETS). This publication is not endorsed or approved by ETS.

Best Practices

Each chapter identifies at least six different activities that support six Best Practices, principles that contribute to excellent language teaching and learning. Identifying Best Practices helps teachers to see, and make explicit for students, how a particular activity will aid the learning process.

Making Use of Academic Content

Materials and tasks based on academic content and experiences give learning real purpose. Students explore real world issues, discuss academic topics, and study content-based and thematic materials.

Organizing Information

Students learn to organize thoughts and notes through a variety of graphic organizers that accommodate diverse learning and thinking styles.

Scaffolding Instruction

A scaffold is a physical structure that facilitates construction of a building. Similarly, scaffolding instruction is a tool used to facilitate language learning in the form of predictable and flexible tasks. Some examples include oral or written modeling by the teacher or students, placing information in a larger framework, and reinterpretation.

Activating Prior Knowledge

Students can better understand new spoken or written material when they connect to the content. Activating prior knowledge allows students to tap into what they already know, building on this knowledge, and stirring a curiosity for more knowledge.

Interacting with Others

Activities that promote human interaction in pair work, small group work, and whole class activities present opportunities for real world contact and real world use of language.

Cultivating Critical Thinking

Strategies for critical thinking are taught explicitly. Students learn tools that promote critical thinking skills crucial to success in the academic world.

1

Academic Life Around the World

Chapter Opener

- ❏ Point out the title of this chapter, "Academic Life Around the World." Ask students to make predictions about what this chapter's theme is likely to be.

- ❏ Have students look at the photo. Explain that this is a picture of a college seminar in the United States. Ask and answer the questions in Connecting to the Topic.

- ❏ Read the quotation or call on a student to read it. Share some of the cultural information about Diogenes with students. Then ask them if they agree or disagree with the statement. Ask them to comment on the importance of education in their home countries.

- ❏ Have students look at the Writing Product. Tell them that, as they work through the chapter, they should keep in mind that this will be the major writing assignment for the chapter.

Content Note

Diogenes Laertius is thought to have lived in the third century A.D. He is best known as a biographer of ancient Greek philosophers. His ten-volume work, *Lives and Opinions of Eminent Philosophers*, is an important source of information on the development of Greek philosophy.

❝ The foundation of every state is the education of its youth. ❞

—Diogenes Laertius
Biographer of Greek philosophers (c. 250)

Chapter Overview

Writing Product

A descriptive paragraph about a classmate

Writing Process

- Interview a classmate.
- Distinguish fact and opinion.
- Create a graphic organizer.
- Learn about topic sentences.
- Connect ideas with *and*, *but*, and *so*.
- Use *also* to add information.
- Learn to revise for content and edit for form.
- Use a writing rubric to evaluate a first draft.

Part 1: Before You Write

Exploring Ideas

Building Vocabulary

Organizing Ideas

Using Graphic Organizers

Writing Topic Sentences

Part 2: Developing Writing Skills

Using *And* to Connect Phrases and Sentences

Using *Also* to Add Information

Using *But* and *So* to Connect Sentences

Writing the First Draft

Part 3: Revising and Editing

Revising for Content

Editing for Form

Evaluating Your Writing

Peer Sharing

Writing the Second Draft

Part 4: Expansion Activities

Writing and Researching

What Do You Think?

Journal Writing

Self-Assessment Log

Exploring Ideas

Best Practice

Activating Prior Knowledge

The expansion activity that follows gives students the opportunity to link prior knowledge to new information they acquire. By thinking about the questions, students build expectations about the coming information, and their prior knowledge on the topic is activated.

 EXPANSION ACTIVITY

- Tell students that they are going to write about academic life. Ask them about the first images or ideas that come to mind when they think about university life.

- Photocopy and distribute **Black Line Master 1**, "Academic Life," on page BLM1 of this Teacher's Edition. Have students answer the questions and discuss their answers as a class.

Content Note

Famous Universities

North and Latin America

Harvard University, Stanford University, Berkeley, Massachusetts Institute of Technology, University of São Paulo, University of Mexico

Europe

Cambridge University, Oxford University, University of Paris, University of Munich, Moscow State University

Asia Pacific

Tokyo University, Australian National University, Seoul National University, Chinese University Hong Kong

Middle East

Alexandria University, American University of Beirut, Amman University, Arabian Gulf University, Damascus University

- Have students look at the photo. Tell students that the man and woman are university students. Ask students what they think is happening in the photo.

Best Practice

Scaffolding Instruction

This chapter makes extensive use of scaffolded instruction. For many students, the idea of interviewing a classmate and then writing a paragraph based on that interview might seem a daunting task. The scaffolding practices employed here help students construct their final product through a series of structured, clear, and authentic activities.

1 **Reviewing Interview Questions**

- Have students read the list of interview questions.

2 **Writing Interview Questions**

- Have students take five minutes to brainstorm a list of questions they would like to ask during their own interviews. They can include any of the questions from their texts in their lists, and they should create at least three new questions.

- You may want to group students in pairs or small groups if they are having trouble working individually.

3 **Sharing Your Interview Questions**

Best Practice

Cultivating Critical Thinking

Activities such as this one require students to critically evaluate their work and make decisions about which questions will lead to valuable information for them to use in their paragraphs.

❏ Note the group icon. Ask students to share some of their interview questions. Write some of the questions on the board as students dictate them to you. Write the questions on the board in the most natural, logical order.

❏ Ask students what they think are the best questions to ask.

❏ After the discussion, allow students time to edit their lists of questions.

EXPANSION ACTIVITY

▪ The aim of this activity is to get students to think of some examples of questions that might be inappropriate in this kind of interview, such as *Do you have a boyfriend or girlfriend? How much money does your father earn? How much do you weigh?*

▪ As a group, discuss why certain questions are inappropriate (e.g., some are too personal or some might make people uncomfortable). Make a list of appropriate and inappropriate interview topics on the board.

4 Interviewing Someone

Best Practice

Interacting with Others

In activities such as this interview, students have the opportunity to interact with others and use language in a meaningful way. Here students put their interview questions into practice with someone other than the teacher and gather genuine responses.

❏ Note the pair icon. Have students write their lists of ten questions in their notebooks or on a piece of paper.

❏ Tell students that they will take notes during the interview and then use these notes to write their paragraph.

❏ You may want to designate pairs, rather than having students choose their partners.

❏ Give students a time limit for their interviews, such as 15 minutes.

❏ Students might want to record their interviews if they have the equipment to do so.

Building Vocabulary

5 Using a Vocabulary Chart

Best Practice

Cultivating Critical Thinking

Activities such as this one will teach students to analyze vocabulary. Here, using a graphic organizer, they analyze vocabulary used in the interviews. The act of completing the chart will help students visualize the different vocabulary categories, and the completed chart will clearly show how the writer organized his or her vocabulary. Working with organizational tools such as this one exposes students to an excellent way of organizing information that they can use in their own vocabulary acquisition.

❏ Note the group icon. Have students look at the vocabulary chart in their books. Ask them how the vocabulary is organized.

❏ Point out that listing words by categories or topics can be an effective way to learn new vocabulary.

 EXPANSION ACTIVITY

▪ The aim of this activity is to have students think of another vocabulary topic related to "Academic Life Around the World," such as school sports, and then organize the vocabulary for that topic into categories.

▪ Using school sports as a model topic, ask students how they would break that topic into vocabulary categories, such as individual sports (swimming), pair sports (tennis), and team sports (football). Elicit other categories, such as indoor and outdoor sports.

- Photocopy and distribute **Black Line Master 2**, "Vocabulary Chart," on page BLM2 of this Teacher's Edition. Have students fill in the vocabulary chart. Ask them to think of as many vocabulary items as they can for each category. Have students share some examples with the class.

Organizing Ideas

Strategy

Facts and Opinions

- After the students have had a chance to read silently, read the text box aloud or call on a student to read it aloud.

- Ask volunteers to give one example of a statement of fact and one of an opinion. Ask another volunteer to explain why one is a fact and the other an opinion.

EXPANSION ACTIVITY

- The aim of this activity is to give students additional practice in identifying facts and opinions about their interests.

- Create two columns on the board. Label one *Fact* and the other *Opinion*.

- Write down a few examples, such as (fact) age, location, time; and (opinion) favorite food, best movie, boring book.

- Ask students to give examples of facts and opinions, and write these on the board.

- Discuss whether each is truly a fact or an opinion.

6 Distinguishing Fact and Opinion

- ❏ Direct the students to the activity with statements from a student's interview with Yara Haider. Review the directions and first example.

- ❏ After students have finished, review the answers with the class.

ANSWER KEY

1. F 2. F 3. F 4. F 5. F 6. F 7. O 8. O 9. F
10. F

Using Graphic Organizers

Strategy

Graphic Organizers

After the students have had a chance to read silently, read the text box aloud or call on a student to read it aloud.

7 Analyzing a Graphic Organizer

Best Practice

Organizing Information

Throughout this book, students will learn to use a variety of graphic organizers to put together their thoughts and ideas before writing. Such tools help students organize information and vocabulary into clear and meaningful chunks. Graphic organizers are particularly effective with more visually oriented and logical learners.

- ❏ Note the group icon. Have students look at the graphic organizer containing notes from the interview in Activity 6. Put students in groups of three to discuss the following questions:

- ❏ The information is organized in several groups. What do the groups represent?

- ❏ How does the diagram show that information is related?

- ❏ What information from the interview is not included in the diagram?

❑ Where should it go? How do you know?

8 Creating a Graphic Organizer

Best Practice

Scaffolding Instruction

One way of scaffolding instruction is to model a task for the students before they are asked to perform it themselves. Modeling gives students concrete ideas of what information is needed and how to supply it in a given situation. Modeling how to fill in the graphic organizer based on the interview in Activity 6 gives students the tools and confidence to proceed on their own.

❑ If students have difficulties distinguishing fact from opinion in their interview questions, encourage them to review Activity 6.

9 Sharing Your Graphic Organizer

❑ Note the pair icon. Allow students time to share their graphic organizers with their partners.

Writing Topic Sentences

Strategy

Functions and Characteristics of a Topic Sentence

After the students have had a chance to read silently, read the text box aloud or call on a student to read it aloud. Encourage students to ask questions about anything they do not understand.

10 Choosing the Best Topic Sentence

❑ Ask volunteers to create other possible topic sentences, and write these on the board.

11 Writing a Draft Topic Sentence

❑ Remind students that their topic sentence should state the main idea of their paragraph. Encourage them to refer to their graphic organizers to identify the main idea.

Developing Cohesion and Clarity

Strategy

Connecting Ideas

After the students have had a chance to read silently, read the text box aloud or call on a student to read it aloud.

1   Analyzing Connectors

Best Practice

Cultivating Critical Thinking

Activities such as these teach a particular critical thinking skill and provide varied opportunities for practicing it. In this case, students are asked to differentiate between new information, results, and contrasting information. The expansion activity after Activity 7 (in this Teacher's Edition) provides more opportunity for synthesizing and applying this skill.

❑ Note the group icon. Direct students to the paragraph about Yara Haider on page 9. Have them circle the words *and*, *but*, *so*, and *also*.

❑ Put the students into small groups and have the groups answer the questions. Make sure the students understand *add*, *result*, and *contrast*.

❑ Make sure students understand that the words *and* and *also* introduce new information, *so* introduces a result, and *but* contrasts information.

USING *AND* TO CONNECT PHRASES AND SENTENCES

■ Have volunteers read the example sentences aloud.

■ Remind students that when *and* connects phrases that have the same subject, there is no need to use a comma before *and*.

2   Connecting Sentences with *And*

❑ Review the directions and first example.

❑ After students have finished, review the answers with the class.

ANSWER KEY

1. Ming Su is 26 years old and comes from Taiwan. 2. Amelia eats breakfast and lunch in the cafeteria. 3. Reiko is 19 years old and likes music a lot. 4. Salma is married and a student. 5. Enrique likes soccer and plays every Saturday. 6. The school offers a good program in business, and its recreational facilities are excellent.

USING *ALSO* TO ADD INFORMATION

■ As part of your instruction, have students read the example sentences aloud.

3   Using *Also* in Sentences

❑ Review the directions and first example.

❑ After students have finished, review the answers with the class.

ANSWER KEY

1. David likes baseball. He also likes rock music. 2. Hamid is tall. He is also very athletic. 3. In her free time, Maddie plays basketball. She also likes to swim. 4. Efraim works part-time. He also takes care of his four children.

4   Writing Sentences with *And* and *Also*

❑ Direct students to use their graphic organizers and notes to construct sentences using *and* and *also*. Ask a volunteer to give an example, and write it on the board.

❑ Review students' work for grammar and coherence. Write some examples on the board.

USING *BUT* AND *SO* TO CONNECT SENTENCES

- As part of your instruction, have students read the example sentences aloud.

- Point out the use of the comma in the example sentences. Remind students that a comma indicates a pause. In sentences with *but* information is being contrasted. A pause, indicated by a comma, helps the reader differentiate between chunks of information.

5 **Using *And* and *But* to Connect Sentences**

- ❏ Review the directions and first example.

- ❏ After students have finished, review the answers with the class.

ANSWER KEY

1. Alberto lives with his sister, and she drives him to school every afternoon. 2. Yara can speak English well, but she needs more writing practice. 3. Western Adult School is in a beautiful location, but it doesn't have very good library facilities. 4. Yara is Syrian, but/and she is studying in Lebanon. 5. Yara's father is proud of her, and he's happy that she's studying in Lebanon.

6 **Using *But* and *So* to Connect Sentences**

- ❏ Review the directions and first example.

- ❏ After students have finished, review the answers with the class.

ANSWER KEY

1. She has to work all day, so she doesn't have time to do all of her homework. 2. He likes his English class, but he doesn't think the American students are very friendly. 3. Her company is opening an office in the United States, so it needs English-speaking workers. 4. She likes academic life, but she is homesick for her family. 5. Pedro wants to work in Japan, so he needs to learn Japanese.

7 **Writing Sentences with *But* and *So***

- ❏ Ask one or two volunteers to look at their interview notes and model a sentence using *but* or *so*. Write these on the board.

- ❏ After students have written their sentences, ask volunteers to share some examples. Write these on the board, and ask students to evaluate them for grammar and sense.

 EXPANSION ACTIVITY

- The aim of this activity is to give students additional practice in writing sentences with *and*, *but*, *so*, and *also*.

- Photocopy and distribute **Black Line Master 3**, "Connecting Sentences," on page BLM3 of this Teacher's Edition. Review the directions and first example.

- Remind the students to pay attention to their use of commas.

- After students have finished, review the answers with the class.

Strategy

Writing a First Draft

Explain the idea of the first draft and have students read the information in the box on page 12 of the Student Book.

ORDERING INFORMATION IN A PARAGRAPH

- Call on a student to read the information about ordering information in a paragraph aloud.

  - Review the difference between facts and opinions.

  - Encourage students to ask any questions they may have.

Writing with Computers

- After the students have had a chance to read silently, read the text aloud or ask a volunteer to read it aloud.

- Elicit from students how to change the line-spacing in their word processing programs. (Format—Paragraph—Line Spacing) on the tool bar.

8 Writing the First Draft

- ❑ To write their first drafts, have students use the graphic organizer and the topic sentence that they created on pages 7 and 8.

- ❑ Emphasize that a first draft is a very rough form of writing. Students should write complete, logical sentences, but they will revise these later. The content is the most important factor in the rough draft.

- ❑ Remind them to try to use connectors like *and*, *so*, *but*, and *also*.

Revising for Content and Editing for Form

Strategy

Revising for Content

- Have a volunteer read the information about revising for content.

- Encourage students to ask questions about anything they may not understand.

- Ask students to describe their own methods for revision.

1 Revising for Content

- ❑ In this activity, students are to look at the writer's ideas and organization. Students should focus on content, organization, and other "macro" issues.

- ❑ Review the questions with students before they revise.

- ❑ **Note to instructor:** The following sample paragraph has been revised for both content and form and should be referred to for both activities 1 and 2.

SAMPLE PARAGRAPH

Wichai Tongkhio is a new member of the English composition class at Amarin Community College. Wichai is 18 years old, and he is originally from a village in the north. In general, Wichai likes life in Bangkok and Amarin Community College, but he doesn't like his dormitory. He is studying business administration, accounting, and English. Wichai plans to visit the United States next summer, so he needs to learn English. In his free time, Wichai plays basketball, and he likes going to the movies.

Strategy

Editing for Form

- Have volunteers read the information about editing for form.

- Answer any questions students might have.

2 Editing for Form

- ❑ In this activity, students are to edit for form. Students should focus on punctuation, spelling, and other "micro" issues. Review the directions with students before they edit.

- ❑ **Note to instructor:** The sample paragraph following activity 1 has been revised for both content and form and should be referred to for both activities 1 and 2.

Evaluating Your Writing

Strategy

Using Rubrics

- Have a volunteer read the information about using rubrics.

- Encourage students to ask questions about anything they may not understand.

3 Using a Rubric

Best Practice

Cultivating Critical Thinking

Activities such as these require students to critically evaluate their own and others' writing based on both set criteria and more general guidelines. Students then make judgments and suggestions on the overall quality of the paragraphs.

❑ Review the rubric with your class. Ask volunteers to give an example of each of the qualities outlined in the *Excellent* category.

❑ Then have students use the rubric to score their writing.

PEER SHARING

■ Have a volunteer read the information aloud.

■ Elicit what might be the advantages of peer sharing when learning how to write well.

4 Peer Sharing

> **Best Practice**
>
> **Interacting with Others**
>
> Activities such as this give students the opportunity to interact with a partner and receive constructive feedback on their writing. Here, students share their writing with a partner who provides a fresh perspective and offers useful comments.

❑ Note the pair icon. Give pairs of students time to exchange papers and read each other's work. Make sure students partner with someone they did not interview.

❑ Emphasize that students should not judge or correct the writing. They should mention the parts of the paragraph that they found most interesting or surprising. Then they should ask questions about sections that are confusing, or tell the writer where, as a reader, they want more information or detail.

5 Writing the Second Draft

❑ Explain the importance of the *second draft*. Have students rewrite their paragraphs based on their peer's comments and their own rubric evaluation from Activity 3.

Best Practice

Making Use of Academic Content

This section of the chapter abounds in content-based, authentic material that gives students experience in publishing, interviewing, reading to improve their writing, writing factual material based on Internet research, and writing in a journal.

1 Sharing Your Writing

❑ You might have students input their paragraphs on the computer and print out multiple copies to share with the class.

2 Making a Class Newsletter

❑ If you have a desktop publishing program, students can use that to create a newsletter with their paragraphs. Otherwise, they can assemble corrected, typewritten copies into a booklet and distribute it to other classes.

3 Interviewing Your Teacher

❑ This is a group writing activity based on an interview with you, the instructor. Encourage students to follow the same process they used for their peer interviews: developing good interview questions, conducting (and taking notes on) the interview, organizing information, identifying the main idea and topic sentence, and using connectors to link information.

Strategy

Reading to Improve Your Writing

■ Call on a student to read aloud the information about reading to improve your writing.

■ Ask students to talk about publications in English that they read. Do they find that reading in English helps them to become better writers?

4 Reading to Improve Your Writing

❑ You can create a reading center for students to improve their ability to read different genres and formats of printed materials. Magazines, newspapers, comic books, and even children's picture books can all be gathered together and displayed in a special area of the room. These provide opportunities for 'quick-and-easy' reading sessions. This will help students get into the habit of reading on a regular basis.

What Do You Think?

Ideally this activity should be done using the Internet. If Internet access is not available to the students, you can provide copies of tabloids or other popular magazines featuring articles about celebrities for students to use.

Strategy

Journal Writing

Have students read the paragraph about journal writing to help them get started with their journals. Discuss the suggestions and remind them that journal writing doesn't have to be grammatically correct or well-organized.

5 Writing in Your Journal

❑ If students do not mind sharing their journals with you, you might read them from time to time and write commentary or other kinds of responses to create a 'dialogue journal.'

Self-Assessment Log

❑ Review the statements in the self-assessment log and then have students complete it.

Experiencing Nature

Chapter Opener

❏ Point out the title of this chapter, "Experiencing Nature." Ask students what they think the title means and to make predictions about what this chapter's theme is likely to be.

❏ Have students look at the photo. Explain that this is a picture of a desert. Ask students whether they find the scene beautiful, and if so, in what ways. Ask and answer the questions in Connecting to the Topic.

❏ Read the quotation or call on a student to read it. Share some of the cultural information about Aristotle with students. Then ask them if they agree or disagree with the statement. Ask them to comment on the importance of nature in their own lives.

❏ Have students look at the description of the Writing Product. Tell them that as they work through the chapter, they should keep in mind that this will be the major writing assignment for the chapter.

Content Note

One of the most famous Greek philosophers, Aristotle, lived from 384 to 322 B.C. He studied under Plato for 20 years. Aristotle had a habit of walking about as he lectured. Thus, his followers became known as the *peripatetics*, meaning "to walk about."

❝ In all things of nature there is something of the marvelous. **❞**

—Aristotle
Greek Philosopher (384 B.C.–322 B.C.)

Chapter Overview

Writing Product

A descriptive paragraph about a painting

Writing Process

- Analyze and discuss paintings.
- Order information from general to specific.
- Group details in spatial order.
- Use descriptive adjectives.
- Use prepositional phrases.
- Use the present continuous.
- Use pronouns and articles.

Part 1: Before You Write

Exploring Ideas

Building Vocabulary

Organizing Ideas

Part 2: Developing Writing Skills

Using Adjectives to Write About Details

Using Prepositional Phrases to Write About Details

Using Pronouns

Using the Present Continuous

Using Articles: *A, An,* and *The*

Part 3: Revising and Editing

Revising for Content

Editing for Form

Evaluating Your Writing

Peer Sharing

Writing the Second Draft

What do You Think?

Part 4: Expansion Activities

Writing and Researching

Journal Writing

Self-Assessment Log

Exploring Ideas

Best Practice

Activating Prior Knowledge

The expansion activity that follows gives students the opportunity to link prior knowledge to new information they acquire. The activity includes questions that will help students form expectations about the coming information. By trying to find answers to these questions, students will activate their prior knowledge on the topic.

 REPRODUCIBLE — **EXPANSION ACTIVITY**

■ The aim of this activity is to have students think and write about nature.

■ Photocopy and distribute **Black Line Master 4**, "Nature," on page BLM4 of this Teacher's Edition.

■ Ask students to think about nature. What are some of the first images or ideas that come to mind?

Content Note

Natural Wonders

North and Latin America

Angel Falls – Venezuela; The Grand Canyon – Arizona, USA; Iguassu Falls – Brazil/Argentina; Niagara Falls – Canada/USA; Paricutin Volcano – Mexico; Amazon River – Latin America

Europe

The Dolomites – Italy; Lake Baikal – Russia; Aletsch Glacier – Switzerland; Fjords – Norway

Asia Pacific

The Great Barrier Reef – Australia; Krakatau Island – Indonesia; Mount Everest – Nepal; Mount Fuji – Japan

Middle East

The Dead Sea – Israel/Jordan; Sand Dunes – Saudi Arabia; Red Sea – Middle East/Africa

Africa

Mount Kilimanjaro – Tanzania; Victoria Falls – Zambia/Zimbabwe; Sahara Desert – North Africa

❑ Have students look at the photo. Tell them they are going to analyze the painting in small groups.

1 Analyzing a Painting

❑ Note the group icon. In small groups, have students use the seven questions to discuss the painting.

❑ After students have finished, have them share their responses with the class.

❑ Share the historical information about the painting with students after they have responded to the questions; then discuss.

ANSWER KEY

Answers may vary. Possible answers:

1. *Watson and the Shark*

2. A shark is a large animal that lives in the ocean. It has many teeth. Sharks eat fish and other animals in the ocean. Sharks are known to attack humans on rare occasions.

3. Watson is the man who is drowning in the foreground of the painting. His clothes have fallen off in the water.

4. There are ten people in the picture.

5. In the painting, there are nine men on a small boat. One man has fallen overboard. Or, perhaps he was stranded and the others have come to rescue him. He is completely naked. The other men are trying to save him from the shark. One man is aiming a spear at the shark.

6. The picture makes me feel anxious. The scene is very dramatic. There is a sense of urgency and fear.

7. I can see many other ships in the background. This may be happening near a city, in a harbor.

Content Note

In 1749 an event took place that served as the inspiration for a great work of art, John Singleton Copley's *Watson and the Shark*. This painting depicts the dramatic scene of a shark attack off the coast of Havana, Cuba. One afternoon, while serving as a crew member on a trading ship, fourteen-year-old orphan Brook Watson hoped to enjoy a solitary swim in the ocean. Suddenly, Watson felt the sharp pain of shark teeth piercing his ankle. As his shipmates rushed to his rescue, the boy struggled to break free from the shark's grip, losing his foot in the battle. In the painting, traces of Watson's blood can be seen in the water and on the shark's mouth.

Brook Watson survived the attack and went on to become a successful statesman, serving as Lord Mayor of London between 1796 and 1797.

Building Vocabulary

Best Practice

Organizing Information

Throughout this book, students will learn to use a variety of graphic organizers to put their thoughts and ideas together before writing. Completing vocabulary charts helps students organize information and vocabulary into clear and meaningful chunks. Graphic organizers are particularly effective with more visually oriented and logical learners.

2 Using a Vocabulary Chart

❑   Have students look at the vocabulary chart in their books. Ask them how the vocabulary is organized. Point out that listing words by categories or topics can be an effective way to learn new vocabulary.

❑   Allow students time to add words to their charts. You might have students return to their groups from Activity 1 for this activity.

❑   After students have finished, review answers with the class.

ANSWER KEY

Answers may vary. Possible answers:

Nouns: foreground, lifeboat, harpoon, fear

Adjectives: realistic

Verbs: drown, aim, save

Other: quickly

3 Using New Vocabulary

❑   Note the group icon. Model or have a volunteer model choosing a noun, such as *oar*, and pointing to it in the picture. Have a volunteer choose an adjective from the list and point to something in the painting that exemplifies that adjective. Have a volunteer choose a verb from the chart and point to a person or thing in the painting that is "doing" the action the verb describes. Then have students, in groups of three, complete the three tasks.

❑   After students have finished, have them share some of their answers with the class.

4 Writing with New Vocabulary

Best Practice

Scaffolding Instruction

This chapter makes extensive use of scaffolded instruction. For many students, the idea of writing a paragraph about a painting might seem very challenging. The scaffolding practices employed here help students construct their final product through a series of structured, clear, and authentic activities.

❑   Review the activity directions with the class.

❑   Model or have a volunteer model creating a sentence using two of the vocabulary words.

- ❑ After students have finished, review answers with the class.

- ❑ Which student used the most vocabulary words from their chart?

ANSWER KEY

Answers may vary. Possible answers:

1. Nine men are crowded into a small <u>rowboat</u>.

2. A <u>naked</u> man is <u>drowning</u> in the <u>harbor</u>.

3. A <u>huge</u> shark with sharp <u>teeth</u> is about to <u>attack</u> the poor man.

4. A man with a <u>rope</u> on his hip and a <u>spear</u> is trying to <u>save</u> the drowning man.

5 **Generating New Vocabulary Through Discussion**

Best Practice

Interacting with Others

In activities such as this discussion, students have the opportunity to interact with others and use language in a meaningful way. Here students discuss their own and others' experiences to generate useful vocabulary.

Best Practice

Activating Prior Knowledge

Activities such as this give students the opportunity to link prior knowledge to new information they acquire through discussion. They can also learn new vocabulary from their partners that may be useful in their writing.

REPRODUCIBLE — EXPANSION ACTIVITY

- ■ Photocopy and distribute **Black Line Master 5**, "Useful Vocabulary," on page BLM5 of this Teacher's Edition before students break into small groups.

- ■ Have students add any new vocabulary words from their discussion to the chart that might be useful in their descriptive paragraphs about a painting.

- ■ Have volunteers give examples of vocabulary words they would add to each category of the BLM.

- ■ Tell students that they can add to this list as they progress through the chapter.

- ❑ Note the group icon. Before students break into small groups to discuss what they know about sharks, you might want to share a few facts about these predatory animals. For example:

  1. There are about 250 species of sharks.

  2. They are one of the oldest animals on the planet – their present form has remained virtually unchanged for millions of years.

  3. They must swim constantly to avoid sinking.

  4. In spite of their reputation for unprovoked attack, only 27 of the 250 known species have definitely been implicated in attacks on humans.

- ❑ You can also direct students' attention to the information about sharks in the box on page 24 of their books.

- ❑ Encourage students to share with their group members any other facts and stories they may know about sharks.

- ❑ Remind students to add any vocabulary words they think might be useful in their writing to their Useful Vocabulary chart.

Organizing Ideas

Strategy

Ordering Information in a Paragraph

■ After the students have had a chance to read silently, read the text box aloud or call on a student to read it aloud.

■ Ask students why it is important to move from general to specific information in a descriptive paragraph. Elicit that the general information gives the reader a context and the specific information adds detail.

6 **Distinguishing General and Specific Information**

❑ Direct students to the paragraph describing *A Sunday on La Grande Jatte*. Have students take turns identifying the sentences that give general information and those that give specific information.

❑ Have students identify which comes first: the general information or the specific information.

ANSWER KEY

Sentences with general information:

A Sunday on La Grande Jatte by Georges Seurat is a picture of a Parisian park on a warm and sunny day.

Although the scene is quite busy, it also seems quiet and peaceful.

Sentences with specific information:

On the left, there is a lake.

Three sailboats are moving on the lake.

Four men and one woman are riding in a canoe.

On the shore, some people are lying on the grass gazing at the water.

In the background, a man is playing a trumpet.

Two soldiers are standing motionless.

On the right, a man and a woman are dressed in elegant clothes.

They are staring at the water.

There is a monkey dancing at their feet.

In the center, a woman is holding an umbrella with one hand and a little girl with the other.

EXPANSION ACTIVITY

■ Create two columns on the board, labeled *General* and *Specific*.

■ Tell students to think about the topic of sports. Write an example in each column, such as (general) *A lot of people enjoy watching sports on TV.*; and (specific) *Soccer is the most popular sport in Italy*.

■ Ask students to give general and specific examples of their own, and write some examples on the board.

■ Discuss whether each is truly general or specific.

7 **Identifying the Topic Sentence**

❑ Review the activity directions with the class.

❑ After students have finished, review the correct answer and discuss why it is the best topic sentence (i.e., it introduces the main idea, it gives some general information about the painting, but it doesn't give any details).

ANSWER KEY

Although the scene is quite busy, it also seems quiet and peaceful.

8 Choosing the Best Topic Sentence

- ❑ Review the activity directions with the class.

- ❑ After students have finished, review the correct answer and again stress that it introduces the main idea, but it doesn't give any details.

ANSWER KEY

Watson and the Shark, by John Singleton Copley, shows a dramatic rescue attempt.

9 Writing General Statements

- ❑ Review the activity directions and the sample sentence.

- ❑ Have students share their general statements with the class. Are they truly general?

ANSWER KEY

Answers may vary. Possible answers:

The painting shows a very frightening scene.

The scene took place many years ago.

10 Writing About Details

- ❑ Review the activity directions and examples.

- ❑ With the class, create a sample sentence using one of the examples.

- ❑ Have students share their sentences with the class. Do they provide detailed information about the painting?

ANSWER KEY

Answers may vary. Possible answers:

Two of the men in the rowboat are reaching for the man in the water.

A shark is about to attack a man in the sea.

The man in the water looks frightened.

One of the men is trying to kill the shark with a spear.

11 Ordering Ideas in a Paragraph

- ❑ Review the activity directions. Explain that students should try to describe one section or aspect of the painting at a time, such as what is going on in the boat or what is happening in the water.

- ❑ Have a few volunteers share their sentences with the class. Discuss whether their organization makes sense.

Developing Cohesion and Clarity

USING ADJECTIVES TO WRITE ABOUT DETAILS

- After the students have had a chance to read silently, read the text and examples aloud or call on students to read aloud.

- Ask volunteers to give examples of using two adjectives connected with *and*.

1 Listing Adjectives

> **Best Practice**
>
> **Cultivating Critical Thinking**
>
> Activities such as these teach a particular critical thinking skill and provide varied opportunities for practicing it. In this case, students are asked to communicate details about the painting, modifying nouns with adjectives. The expansion activity after Activity 6 provides more opportunity for synthesizing and applying this skill.

- Note the pair icon. Review the activity directions and example.

- You may want to pair weaker students with stronger ones for this activity.

- Encourage students to list as many adjectives for each noun as they can.

- After students have finished, review answers with the class.

ANSWER KEY

Answers may vary. Possible answers:

1. the boat: small, overloaded, wooden 2. the men in the boat: tense, scared, worried 3. the weather: dark, gray, windy 4. the shark: huge, frightening, angry 5. the man in the water: pale, lifeless, naked 6. the water: clear, choppy, cold

2 Using Adjectives in Sentences

- Review the activity directions and first example.

- After students have finished, review possible answers with the class.

ANSWER KEY

Answers may vary. Possible answers:

1. The small, overloaded boat looks like it's going to sink. 2. The men in the boat are tense and scared. 3. The weather looks dark and gray.
4. There is a huge, frightening shark in the water.
5. The man in the water looks pale and lifeless.
6. The water looks clear and cold.

USING PREPOSITIONAL PHRASES TO WRITE ABOUT DETAILS

- As part of your instruction, have students read the example sentences aloud.

- Model or have volunteers model using the prepositional phrases of location to describe objects in the classroom.

3 Identifying Prepositional Phrases of Location

- Review the activity directions. You might want to identify the first prepositional phrase of location with the students.

- After students have finished, review the answers with the class.

ANSWER KEY

A Sunday on La Grande Jatte by Georges Seurat is a picture of a Parisian park on a warm and sunny day. Although the scene is quite busy, it also seems quiet and peaceful. <u>On the left</u>, there is a lake. Three sailboats are moving <u>on the lake</u>. Four men and one woman are riding <u>in a canoe</u>. <u>On the shore</u>, some people are lying <u>on the grass</u> gazing at the water. In the background, a man is playing a trumpet. Two soldiers are standing motionless. On the right, a man and a woman are dressed in elegant clothes. They are staring at the water. There is a monkey dancing at their feet. In the center, a woman is holding an umbrella with one hand and a little girl with the other.

4 Adding Prepositional Phrases to Sentences

❑ Review the activity directions and first example. Elicit that the phrase tells where the tree is.

❑ After students have finished, review the answers with the class.

ANSWER KEY

1. *In the center* is the tree of life. 2. Two children are standing *under the tree of life*. 3. Several birds are flying *out of the tree*. 4. On the right are two people sitting *at a table*. 5. *To the left* a man, a woman, and baby are in a boat. 6. *To the right* is a smaller tree.

5 Writing Sentences with Prepositional Phrases

Best Practice

Scaffolding Instruction

Activities such as these employ the practice of scaffolded instruction, giving students multiple opportunities for participation in authentic activities that are both predictable and flexible. In this and the next activity, students are asked to apply what they have learned about prepositional phrases. The expansion activity after Activity 6 gives students the opportunity to apply what they've learned to a real-life situation.

❑ Review the activity directions.

❑ After students have finished, ask several students to share their sentences with the

class. Have the class identify the prepositional phrase in each.

❑ Write some examples on the board.

ANSWER KEY

Answers may vary. Possible answers:

1. There is a potted plant in the center of the table. 2. A bird is perched on a branch of the tree. 3. Two human figures are standing in the branches of the tree.

6 Writing Sentences with Prepositions of Location

❑ Review the activity directions. Ask a volunteer to create a sample sentence. Ask others to identify the details and the prepositional phrase(s) the volunteer used.

❑ After students have finished, ask several students to share their sentences with the class.

❑ Write some examples on the board.

ANSWER KEY

Answers may vary. Possible answers:

1. A shark is near the man in the water.
2. The man's right arm is raised above the water.
3. The man's legs are under the water.
4. The shark's tail is behind the boat.
5. A man in the boat is aiming a spear at the shark.

Best Practice

Making Use of Academic Content

The following expansion activity contains real-world, authentic material that gives students experience in writing descriptive sentences, using adjectives and prepositional phrases to improve their writing.

EXPANSION ACTIVITY

- Tear out pages from magazines that contain images. Distribute one page to each pair of students.

- Have students write at least five descriptive sentences about their image.

- Remind students to use adjectives and prepositional phrases in their sentences.

- Have students show their image to their classmates and read some of their sentences.

- Write some of the best sentences on the board.

USING PRONOUNS

- Review and discuss the subject/object pronouns chart with the class.

- You might want to model a sentence about the class, such as *[Name] is a student. / She is a student; I am pointing to the door. / I am pointing to it.* Ask a volunteer to write the sentences on the board.

- Have students identify the subject pronoun and the object pronoun in each example.

- You may need to give other examples to make sure students understand the difference between subject and object pronouns.

7 Identifying Pronouns

- ❑ Review the activity directions.

- ❑ After students have finished, review answers with the class.

- ❑ Ask students whether each is a subject or object pronoun.

ANSWER KEY

It (SP) refers to *the scene*.

They (SP) refers to *a man and a woman*.

8 Changing Nouns to Pronouns

Best Practice

Interacting with Others

Activities such as this give students the opportunity to interact with a partner and receive constructive feedback on their work. Here, students share their modified paragraphs with a partner, who evaluates it according to his or her own understanding of pronouns.

- ❑ Review the activity directions. Remind students that they can look at the Using Pronouns chart on page 30 of their books to see a list of subject and object pronouns.

- ❑ After students have finished, have them compare their modified paragraphs with those of a classmate.

- ❑ Call on students to read some of their sentences in which they made a pronoun change. Did they make a subject or object pronoun change? What noun does it represent or refer to? Write some examples on the board.

SAMPLE PARAGRAPH

The painting *Snow Hill and Drum Bridge at Meguro* is by Hiroshige. **He** painted *Snow Hill and Drum Bridge at Meguro* in 1857. **It** is a winter scene. In the middle of the painting, there is a stone bridge over a small river. Although it is winter, the water in the river isn't frozen. **It** is flowing peacefully. There are several people on the bridge. **They** are walking through the deep snow. Some of the people are carrying heavy loads. There are also many trees in the painting. The trees are white because **they** are covered in snow. In the picture, it is night time. The night is cloudless and many stars are shining in the sky. I like this painting because the scene is calm and quiet.

USING THE PRESENT CONTINUOUS

- After the students have had a chance to read silently, read the text and examples aloud, or call on students to read them aloud.

9 Identifying the Present Continuous

- ❑ Review the activity directions.
- ❑ After students have finished, review answers with the class.

ANSWER KEY

is flowing, are walking, are carrying, are shining

10 Writing the –ing Form of Verbs

- ❑ Review the Spelling Rules for Adding –ing to a Verb.
- ❑ Review the activity directions and first example.
- ❑ After students have finished, review answers with the class.

ANSWER KEY

1. swimming 2. staring 3. trying 4. throwing
5. standing 6. attacking 7. looking 8. biting
9. seeing 10. referring

USING ARTICLES: *A, AN*, AND *THE*

- Review the indefinite/definite articles chart with the class.
- Have several volunteers create sentences about things in the classroom using definite/indefinite articles.

11 Adding Articles to Sentences

- ❑ Review the activity directions and first example.
- ❑ After students have finished, review answers with the class.

ANSWER KEY

There is 1 *a* large tree in the middle. Two children are standing under 2 *the* tree, and two children are climbing in 3 *the* tree. 4 *The* children are waving. On the left is 5 *a* man and 6 *a* woman in 7 *a* boat. 8 *The* man is fishing. 9 *The* woman is holding 10 *a* child. 11 *A* large bird is flying over 12 *the* boat. To the right is 13 *a* smaller tree. Two people are sitting under 14 *the* tree at 15 *a* table. On 16 *the* table is 17 *a* plant.

12 Writing the First Draft

- ❑ Have students write their first drafts of a paragraph about the painting, *Watson and the Shark*.
- ❑ Remind them to use their notes from Activity 6 and to use present continuous to tell what is happening.
- ❑ Emphasize that a first draft is a very rough form of writing. Students should write complete, logical sentences, but they will revise these later. The content is the most important factor in the rough draft.

Revising for Content and Editing for Form

1 Revising for Content

- ❏ Review the activity directions with the class.

- ❏ Remind students that this is a revision for content and organization, and they shouldn't be overly concerned with detail.

- ❏ After students have finished, review possible changes with the class. For this first activity focus on the order of sentences.

SAMPLE PARAGRAPH

(Only revised for content. Still contains sentence-level errors.)

The Starry Night is the painting by Vincent van Gogh, a Dutch artist. Nature is very important in this picture. The sky is very big. The sky is beautiful. There are many stars in the sky. In the front of the painting are some tall, curving trees. They are blowing in the wind. In the back are some rolling mountains. In the center is a church. There are some houses and buildings around a church. The stars, trees, and mountains look like they are moving. Our eyes follow their shapes up, around, down, and back again, like a ride on a roller coaster.

2 Editing for Form

- ❏ Review the activity directions with the class.

- ❏ Remind students to focus on form: articles, pronouns, and other "micro" issues. You might want to review guidelines with students before they edit.

- ❏ After students have finished, have several students share the changes they made with the class.

SAMPLE PARAGRAPH

The Starry Night is a painting by the Dutch artist, Vincent van Gogh. Nature is very important in this picture. The most important element is the big, beautiful sky with many stars. In the foreground of the painting are some tall, curving trees, and in the background are some rolling mountains. In the center is a church. There are some houses and buildings around the church. The stars, trees, and mountains look like they are moving. Our eyes follow their shapes up, around, down, and back again, like a ride on a roller coaster.

Evaluating Your Writing

3 Using a Rubric

Best Practice

Cultivating Critical Thinking

Activities such as these require students to critically evaluate their own and others' writing based on both set criteria and more general guidelines. Students then make judgments and suggestions on the overall quality of the paragraphs.

- ❏ Review the rubric with your class. Ask volunteers to give an example of each of the qualities outlined in the *Excellent* category.

- ❏ Then have students use the rubric to score their writing.

4 Peer Sharing

Best Practice

Interacting with Others

Activities such as this give students the opportunity to interact with a partner and receive constructive feedback on their writing. Here, students share their writing with a partner, who evaluates it according to his or her own understanding of good writing practices. Students also get to see how their work is similar to and different from their peers' work.

❑ Note the pair icon. Give students time to exchange papers and read each other's work.

❑ Students should compare their paragraphs and discuss how they are similar or different.

❑ Have a volunteer pair of students share their results with the class.

5 **Writing the Second Draft**

❑ Have students rewrite their paragraph based on their own rubric evaluation from Activity 3 and what they've learned in this chapter.

❑ Collect student paragraphs and make comments and corrections.

❑ Return students' paragraphs so they can answer the questions.

Writing with Computers

■ After the students have had a chance to read silently, read the text aloud or ask a volunteer to read it aloud.

■ Ask students to share experiences with reviewing their revisions. Is it something they do already?

Best Practice

Cultivating Critical Thinking

Activities such as this one require students to analyze art. In this activity, they compare and contrast two pieces of art. They are also asked to evaluate the art in terms of their own tastes. These activities prepare students for the more open-ended activities that follow.

What Do You think?

Analyzing Paintings

■ Review the activity directions with the class.

■ Discuss the questions as a class. Make sure students give reasons for their answers.

ANSWER KEY

Answers may vary. Sample answers:

1. They both show groups of people.

2. *The Tree of Life* by Georges Liautaud and *Watson and the Shark* by John Singleton Copley are the most different. *The Tree of Life* is very abstract, and *Watson and the Shark* is realistic.

3. *A Sunday on La Grande Jatte* and *Snow Hill and Drum Bridge at Meguro* are the most similar. Both show people in nature. They are also both soft and pretty.

4. Students' answers will vary.

5. Students' answers will vary.

Best Practice

Making Use of Academic Content

This section of the chapter abounds in content-based, authentic material that gives students experience in writing descriptive paragraphs about scenery, making a travel brochure, writing in a journal, and researching a painting.

1 **Writing About Scenery**

❏ Review the activity directions with the class.

❏ Provide an art album or postcards from a museum for students to use as a stimulus for this activity. They could also search for paintings on the Internet.

❏ Students can use the writing samples and suggestions throughout this chapter as models to write a description/critique of the piece they choose.

2 **Matching the Picture to the Paragraph**

❏ Note the group icon. Read the directions aloud, or have a student read the directions aloud.

❏ Gather the copies of artwork that students used to complete Activity 1. Display them in front of the class and then read students' descriptions of the artwork in random order. Have the class match the descriptions with the artwork.

3 **Making a Travel Brochure**

❏ Bring in samples of travel brochures that students can use as models for this activity.

❏ Tell students to use sentence connectors to combine different facts in one sentence.

4 **Writing in Your Journal**

❏ If students seem to have difficulty with either activity, suggest that they generate their own ideas for journal topics as long as they are related to the theme of the chapter.

5 **Researching a Painting**

❏ Review the activity directions with the class.

❏ Ideally this activity should be done using the Internet. If Internet access is not available to the students, you can provide art history books.

❏ Ask students to share some of the vocabulary they learned with the class.

Self-Assessment Log

❏ Review the statements in the self-assessment log and then have students complete it.

3

Living to Eat or Eating to Live?

Chapter Opener

- ❏ Point out the title of this chapter, "Living to Eat or Eating to Live?" Ask students what they think the title means and to make predictions about what this chapter's theme is likely to be.

- ❏ Have students look at the photo. Explain that this is a picture of a *buffet*, or a meal put on a table for people to serve themselves. Ask students whether they find the different foods mouthwatering and to explain why. Ask and answer the questions in Connecting to the Topic.

- ❏ Read the quotation or call on a student to read it. Share some of the cultural information about Anthelme Brillat-Savarin with students. Then ask them if they agree or disagree with the statement. Ask them to comment on the importance of food in their own lives.

- ❏ Have students look at the Writing Product. Tell them that as they work through the chapter, they should keep in mind that this will be the major writing assignment for the chapter.

Content Note

Considered by many to be the greatest gastronome (a connoisseur of good food and drink; a gourmet) the world has ever known, Brillat-Savarin lived from 1755 to 1826. This Frenchman was famous for his test dinners where he judged guests based on their reactions and comments to skillfully prepared meals. His masterpiece is considered to be *La Physiologie du Gout* (The Physiology of Taste).

❝ Tell me what you eat, and I will tell you what you are. **❞**

—Anthelme Brillat-Savarin
French politician and food writer (1755–1826)

Chapter Overview

Writing Product

A descriptive paragraph about holiday foods

Writing Process

- Order information from general to specific.
- Create a graphic organizer showing different levels of detail.
- Use count and noncount nouns.
- Give examples with *such as.*
- Use appositives.
- Punctuate lists and appositives.
- Form plural nouns.
- Spell third-person singular verbs.

Part 1: Before You Write

Exploring Ideas

Building Vocabulary

Organizing Ideas

Using Graphic Organizers

Part 2: Developing Writing Skills

Count and Noncount Nouns

Giving Examples with *Such as*

Using Appositives

Part 3: Revising and Editing

Revising for Content

Editing for Form

Evaluating Your Writing

Peer Sharing

Writing the Second Draft

What do You Think?

Part 4: Expansion Activities

Writing and Researching

Journal Writing

Self-Assessment Log

Exploring Ideas

Best Practice

Activating Prior Knowledge

The expansion activity that follows gives students the opportunity to activate prior knowledge about their experiences with food in preparation for writing about holiday food. They are asked to think of foods they like and dislike, foods from their own and other countries, and holiday dishes. They will build on this information in the ensuing activities.

 EXPANSION ACTIVITY

- Tell students that they are going to think and write about food. Ask: What is the first thing that comes to mind?

- Photocopy and distribute **Black Line Master 6**, "Food," on page BLM6 of this Teacher's Edition. Have students answer the questions and then discuss answers as a class.

Content Note

Famous Dishes

Brazil – fejouada; Switzerland – fondue; Germany – wiener schnitzel; Morocco – couscous; Japan – sushi; China – dim sum; U.S. – fried chicken; Spain – paella; Lebanon – schwarma

Content Note

Kwanzaa

Kwanzaa is an African-American celebration that focuses on the traditional African values of family, community responsibility, commerce, and self-improvement. It is celebrated around the same time as, but is not a substitute for, Christmas.

1   Describing Holiday Foods

- ❑   Note the pair icon. In pairs, have students use the questions to discuss the photograph.

- ❑   Start the discussion by telling students that this scene shows a group of people celebrating a special occasion.

- ❑   After students have finished, review their answers with the class.

ANSWER KEY

They are celebrating Kwanzaa.

2   Free Writing

- ❑   Give students five minutes to write in their journals about typical foods they eat every day.

- ❑   Remind them to write as much as they can in the given amount of time without worrying about spelling or grammar.

- ❑   Ask a few volunteers to share what they've written with the class.

3   Discussing Your Free Write

- ❑   In groups of three, have students share what they have written.

- ❑   You may want to start a chart on the board to record students' ideas. Use the chart shown on page 42 of the Student Book as a model.

- ❑   Ask students to identify similarities and differences in what their peers eat every day.

4   Writing About a Holiday

- ❑   After the students have had a chance to silently read the paragraph about Thanksgiving, read the text aloud or call on a student to read it aloud. You might need to explain what some of these foods are.

❑ Students should have no trouble thinking of special holiday foods from their home countries.

❑ To get them started, you may want to share foods typically eaten on one of your own favorite holidays.

5 Comparing Holiday Foods with Regular Food

❑ Review the activity directions with the class.

❑ To make the sentences more interesting, encourage students to write about specific foods and dishes that they eat on holidays.

❑ After students have finished, review answers with the class. Ask if students are familiar with the foods others mention. Write some of the best sentences on the board.

Building Vocabulary

6 Using a Vocabulary Chart

Best Practice

Cultivating Critical Thinking

Activities such as this one will teach students to analyze vocabulary using a graphic organizer. The act of completing the chart will help students visualize the different vocabulary categories and encourage them to associate words with both meanings and functions. Working with organizational tools such as this one exposes students to an excellent way of organizing information that they can use in their own vocabulary acquisition.

❑ Have students look at the vocabulary chart on page 44 of their books. Ask them how the vocabulary is organized. Point out that listing words by categories or topics can be an effective way to learn new vocabulary.

❑ Allow students time to list the underlined words in their charts.

❑ After students have finished, review answers with the class.

ANSWER KEY

Nouns: mixture, specialty

Verbs: celebrate, mix

Adjectives: special, traditional

Other: traditionally, especially

7 Adding Words to the Vocabulary Chart

❑ Note the group icon. In small groups, have students share the sentences they wrote in Activity 5.

❑ Have students write any vocabulary that is new to them in the chart from Activity 6. Encourage them to both use a dictionary to look up the meanings of new words, and to ask the authors about the meanings of new terms.

❑ You may want to check students' charts for spelling and proper categorization.

8 Generating New Vocabulary Through Discussion

Best Practice

Interacting with Others

In activities such as this discussion, students have the opportunity to interact with others and use language in a meaningful way. Here students get to share information about typical foods they eat.

❑ Note the group icon. Encourage students to share other information they may know about food in their groups.

❑ Remind students to answer the questions and note any vocabulary they think might be useful in their writing on their vocabulary chart.

EXPANSION ACTIVITY

- Photocopy and distribute **Black Line Master 7**, "Useful Vocabulary," on page BLM7 of this Teacher's Edition. Print and distribute Useful Vocabulary before students start this activity. This chart will give students a convenient place to organize their vocabulary. Go over the directions with the class.

- Encourage students to describe the foods listed in Activities 4 and 5 and how they're prepared.

- Have students write down any useful vocabulary in their charts. Go over the different categories in the chart and point out that some words may be listed in more than one category (e.g., kabobs in both *Nouns* and *Foods which contain meat).*

Organizing Ideas

Best Practice

Scaffolding Instruction

This chapter makes extensive use of scaffolded instruction. In the following activities, students learn how to order information in a descriptive paragraph and write topic sentences before writing a paragraph on their own. This helps students construct their final product through a series of structured, clear, and authentic activities.

ORDERING INFORMATION IN A PARAGRAPH

- After the students have had a chance to read silently, read the text box aloud or call on students to read it aloud.

- Ask students why it is important to move from general to specific information in a descriptive paragraph. Elicit that the general information gives the reader a context and the specific information adds detail.

- Review the difference between a personal opinion or idea and a fact. Ask students to identify each in the last sentence of the sample paragraph.

9 Ordering Ideas in a Paragraph

- ❏ Review the activity directions with the class.

- ❏ After students have finished, review answers with the class. Have students identify whether each sentence is general in nature (could be true of any holiday) or specific to Thanksgiving.

- ❏ Read the five sentences aloud as a paragraph. Does the paragraph move from general to specific? Does the paragraph end with a personal opinion or idea?

ANSWER KEY

2; 4; 5; 1; 3

Using Graphic Organizers

Best Practice

Organizing Information

Throughout this book, students learn to use a variety of graphic organizers to put together their thoughts and ideas before writing. Activities 6 and 8 help students organize information and vocabulary into clear and meaningful chunks. They are particularly effective with more visually oriented and logical learners.

- ❏ Ask students to give examples of graphic organizers that they've already used in this chapter.

ANSWER KEY

The vocabulary chart in Activities 6 and 8

10 Analyzing a Graphic Organizer

- ❑ Note the group icon. Have students look at the graphic organizer containing notes about Thanksgiving.

- ❑ You might want to put the students into small groups to answer the questions before discussing them as a class.

- ❑ Ask volunteers for more information that could be added to the chart. Ask students where it would go and why.

11 Creating a Graphic Organizer

Best Practice

Scaffolding Instruction

One way of scaffolding instruction is to model a task for the students before they are asked to perform it themselves. Modeling gives students concrete examples of what information is needed and how to supply it in a given situation. Modeling how to fill in the graphic organizer in Activity 10 gives students the tools and confidence to proceed on their own.

- ❑ Review the activity directions with the class.

- ❑ This activity can be done by the class on the board with students volunteering information about one holiday, or have students work in groups on different holidays. Group students by their experience with a common holiday.

- ❑ Have a representative from each group draw their graphic organizer on the board for the class. Allow students to comment and ask questions.

Writing Topic Sentences

Strategy

The Topic Sentence

Review the statements with the class. Have them look back at the paragraph about Thanksgiving on page 43 of their books and identify the topic sentence.

12 Choosing the Best Topic Sentence

- ❑ Review the activity directions with the class.

- ❑ After students have finished, review answers with the class. How are the sentences they chose as the topic sentence the most general? What is the main idea that is being communicated?

ANSWER KEY

On Thanksgiving Day, Americans remember the first Thanksgiving feast of the early American Colonists.

13 Writing a Draft Topic Sentence

Best Practice

Interacting with Others

Activities such as this give students the opportunity to interact with a partner and receive constructive feedback on their work. Here, students share their topic sentences and graphic organizers with a partner who evaluates it based on the questions in his or her book. In this way, they can get concrete feedback about how well they are communicating.

- ❑ Note the pair icon. Review the activity directions with the class.

- ❑ Remind students that their topic sentence should state the main idea of their paragraph. Encourage them to refer to their graphic organizers to identify the main idea.

- ❑ After students have finished, have them work with a partner to answer the questions.

Developing Cohesion and Clarity

COUNT AND NONCOUNT NOUNS

- Review the chart of count and noncount nouns with the class.

- Elicit examples of count and noncount nouns students can see in the classroom: *I see one pair of jeans; Jeans are made of cotton.*

1 Distinguishing Count and Noncount Nouns

Best Practice

Cultivating Critical Thinking

Activities such as these teach a particular critical thinking skill and provide varied opportunities for practicing it. In this case, students are asked to distinguish between count and noncount nouns. The expansion activity after Activity 2 provides more opportunity for synthesizing and applying this skill.

- ❏ Note the group icon. Review the activity directions.

- ❏ Have the students work in small groups. Encourage students to discuss problematic nouns as a group before they resort to using a dictionary.

- ❏ After students have finished, write students' examples in three columns on the board: *Count*, *Noncount*, and *Both*. Students' answers will vary.

2 Categorizing Foods

- ❏ Note the group icon. Have students work in mixed groups—stronger with weaker students. Review the activity directions and example.

- ❏ Have students work with their group to determine what all the different foods are. If they are truly stuck, they can use a search engine or dictionary.

ANSWER KEY

Chinese: chow mein, dim sum, fried rice, spring rolls

Middle Eastern: baklava, hummus, kufta kabob, tabouleh

Indian: curry, paneer, saag, samosas

EXPANSION ACTIVITY

- Tell students they are going to work with their group to determine if the foods they just discussed are count nouns, noncount nouns, or both.

- After students have finished, write students' examples in three columns on the board: *Count*, *Noncount*, and *Both*.

GIVING EXAMPLES WITH *SUCH AS*

- After the students have had a chance to read silently, read the text box and examples aloud, or call on students to read them aloud.

- Invite volunteers to rephrase the sample sentence, substituting the name of a holiday in their home country and food they eat.

3 Writing Sentences with *Such As*

- ❏ Review the activity directions and first example.

- ❏ After students have finished, review possible answers with the class.

- ❏ Ask students to mention other dishes they know, creating sentences with *such as*.

ANSWER KEY

1. Chinese restaurants serve many wonderful dishes such as fried rice, dumplings, and spring rolls.

2. In Chinese restaurants, you can try delicious dishes such as chow mein, dim sum, and fried rice.

3. Students' answers will vary.

4 **Writing Sentences with *Such As***

❑ Review the activity directions.

❑ Have pairs of students take turns reading their sentences to each other.

ANSWER KEY

Answers may vary. Possible answers:

Special dishes are often prepared on important occasions such as weddings and funerals.

USING APPOSITIVES

■ Remind students that commas indicate pauses.

■ As part of your instruction, have students read the example sentences aloud.

5 **Combining Sentences with Appositives**

❑ Review the activity directions and first example.

❑ After students have finished, review the answers with the class.

ANSWER KEY

1. A typical Middle Eastern dish is falafel, a mixture of fried chickpeas and spices. 2. We like to eat fajitas, slices of chicken or beef wrapped in a tortilla with fried peppers and onions. 3. My grandmother is famous for her tempura, a traditional Japanese preparation of shellfish and vegetables. 4. A favorite Iranian dish is fesenjan, chicken in a spicy pomegranate sauce.

6 **Writing Sentences with Appositives**

❑ Review the activity directions.

❑ After students have finished, review the answers with the class.

❑ Write some of the best examples on the board.

ANSWER KEY

Answers may vary. Possible answers:

Tamales, a typical Mexican dish, are very popular on Christmas.

On New Year's Eve, I like to drink eggnog, a spicy drink made with eggs, milk, spices, and rum.

7 **Writing the First Draft**

❑ Have students write their first drafts of a paragraph about holiday foods.

❑ Remind students to use the name of the holiday and the topic sentence they wrote earlier in their graphic organizer.

❑ Emphasize that a first draft is a very rough form of writing. Students should write complete, logical sentences, but they will revise these later. The content is the most important factor in the rough draft.

Revising for Content and Editing for Form

1 Revising for Content

❑ Review the activity directions with the class.

❑ Remind students that this is a revision for content and organization and they shouldn't be concerned about detail.

❑ After students have finished, review possible changes with the class. For this first activity focus on the use of *such as* and appositives. Ignore grammar and spelling errors for now.

SAMPLE PARAGRAPH

Special Christmas Foods

Christmas is an important holiday for many people. People in North America prepares many special Christmas foods from all over the world. Many Christmas specialties, such as fruitcake and eggnog, come from Great Britain. North Americans make fruitcaks with fruites nuts and liquors. Eggnog, a drink of eggs, milk, and sometimes rum, is a very creamy and delicious drink. Americans also eat a lot of Christmas cookies. I love the many special Christmas foods.

EDITING FOR FORM: USING COMMAS IN LISTS

▪ As part of your instruction, first read the example sentences aloud for the students. Direct their attention to the slight pauses where commas occur.

▪ Then ask volunteers to read the example sentences aloud.

2 Adding Commas

❑ Review the activity directions and first example.

❑ After students have finished, review the answers with the class. You might want to have a student write an answer on the board and then read it aloud for the class.

ANSWER KEY

1. Subs, large sandwiches filled with meat, cheese, and vegetables, are popular in the United States.
2. Americans often eat hot dogs, pork, or beef sausages on the Fourth of July.
3. Thais love to eat foods with different tastes such as hot, sour, sweet, and spicy.
4. For lunch, I often have tabouleh, a Middle Eastern salad made from parsley, mint, tomatoes, and wheat.
5. The Italian restaurant near my house serves pasta, pizza, and delicious minestrone soup.
6. Spaghetti, an Italian noodle dish, is popular in North America.

3 Forming Plural Nouns

❑ With the class, review Appendix 1 on page 181 of their books.

❑ Review the activity directions and first example.

ANSWER KEY

1. cookies 2. oranges 3. dishes 4. pancakes
5. cherries 6. dishes 7. tomatoes 8. knives
9. servings 10. boxes

4 Spelling Third-Person Singular Verbs

❑ Review the activity directions and first example.

ANSWER KEY

1. misses 2. watches 3. cooks 4. eats 5. hurries
6. washes 7. drinks 8. dries

Writing with Computers

- After the students have had a chance to read silently, read the text aloud or call on students to read it aloud.

- Discuss students' experiences with spell checkers on computers. Do they use them often? Do the spell checkers catch all mistakes?

5 Editing for Form

❑ Review the activity directions with the class.

❑ Remind students to focus on form: punctuation (commas) and spelling (plural nouns).

❑ After students have finished, review possible changes with the class.

SAMPLE PARAGRAPH

Special Christmas Foods

Christmas is an important holiday for many people. People in North America prepare many special Christmas foods from all over the world. Many Christmas specialties, such as fruitcake and eggnog, come from Great Britain. North Americans make fruitcakes with fruits, nuts, and liquors. Eggnog, a drink of eggs, milk, and sometimes rum, is a very creamy and delicious drink. Americans also eat a lot of Christmas cookies. I love the many special Christmas foods.

Evaluating Your Writing

6 Using a Rubric

Best Practice

Cultivating Critical Thinking

Activities such as this one require students to critically evaluate their own and others' writing based on both set criteria and more general guidelines. Students then make judgments and suggestions on the overall quality of the paragraphs.

❑ Review the rubric with your class. Using the paragraph about Thanksgiving on Student Book page 45, ask students to evaluate it based on the first criteria: **Content** – *Paragraph presents enough information about a holiday and its foods so that the reader has a clear idea of both*.

❑ Then have students use the rubric to score their writing.

7 Peer Sharing

Best Practice

Interacting with Others

Activities such as these give students the opportunity to interact with a partner and receive immediate, constructive feedback on their writing. Students have the chance to discuss what they intended to communicate in writing, and to identify specifically how they did or did not succeed. In the next activity, they get to rewrite their paragraphs, incorporating all the information they've gathered.

❑ Note the pair icon. Use the suggestions in the Student Book on peer sharing.

❑ Give pairs of students time to exchange papers and read each other's work.

❑ Students can write comments in the margins of their partners' papers.

❑ Pairs can then reconvene and give each other verbal feedback, explaining the main points of their written comments.

8 Writing the Second Draft

❑ Have students rewrite their paragraphs based on their own rubric evaluation from Activity 6 and what they've learned in their peer conference.

❑ Students should use correct form and grammar.

❑ Collect student paragraphs and make comments and corrections.

❑ Students may be overwhelmed by the corrections and comments on their papers. You might choose to simply circle errors of grammar and form and encourage students to correct those errors themselves. You might give some comments at the end of their paragraphs about the organization and flow of ideas.

❑ Return students' paragraphs so they can answer the questions.

9 Summarizing Your Strengths and Challenges

Best Practice

Cultivating Critical Thinking

Activities such as this one require students to critically evaluate their own work using the teacher's comments and analyze what they do well and what they need to work on.

❑ Review the activity directions with the class.

❑ To instill confidence in students, you might walk around the class during this activity, briefly discussing with each student some of their strengths and what areas need improvement.

❑ More extensive counseling can be conducted individually.

What Do You Think?

Yin and Yang Foods

■ Review the activity directions with the class.

■ Have students use the prompts in this activity to write in their journals.

■ Students can use their writing as the basis for discussion with a partner.

■ Ask volunteers to share some of their writings with the class.

Best Practice

Making Use of Academic Content

This section of the chapter abounds in content-based, authentic material that gives students experience in writing descriptive paragraphs about holidays and special occasions, writing in a journal, writing a recipe, and researching a holiday.

1 Sharing Your Writing and Pictures

- ❑ Review the activity directions with the class.
- ❑ You might model a presentation about a holiday in your own country as a stimulus for this activity.
- ❑ Allow each student time to share his or her paragraph and supporting artwork with the class.
- ❑ Make a list of the different holidays and their corresponding countries on the board.

2 Writing About Special Occasions

- ❑ Note the pair icon. Review the activity directions with the class.
- ❑ Use the questions and prompts in the student book to have two or more students write about the same holiday or celebration. Each student will have his or her own perspective. Have them exchange papers and comment on the differences and similarities.
- ❑ Ask volunteers to share their descriptions with the class.

3 Writing in Your Journal

- ❑ Review the activity directions with the class.
- ❑ The topics in the Student Book can be used as prompts for journal writing, but students should be encouraged to generate their own ideas.

4 Writing a Recipe

- ❑ Review the activity directions with the class.
- ❑ Discuss students' experiences with recipes. Do they use them? Where do they find them? Do they prefer ones with pictures?
- ❑ Have students use the tabouleh recipe on page 56 in the Student Book as a model for writing their own recipes. The recipes can then be gathered and bound together in a class cookbook. The cookbook can be used for a class party.

5 Researching a Holiday

- ❑ Review the activity directions with the class.
- ❑ Ideally this activity should be done using the Internet. You can give students a keyword search to use: *[name of country] holiday food*.
- ❑ If Internet access is not available to the students, encourage them to use the library.

Self-Assessment Log

- ❑ Review the statements in the self-assessment log and then have students complete it.

In the Community

Chapter Opener

❏ Point out the title of this chapter, "In the Community." Ask students what they think the title means and to make predictions about what this chapter's theme is likely to be.

❏ Have students look at the photo. Explain that this is a picture of part of a modern city. Ask students whether they find this community attractive, and why. Ask and answer the questions in Connecting to the Topic.

❏ Read the quotation or call on a student to read it. Share some of the cultural information about Martin Luther King, Jr. with students. Then ask them if they agree or disagree with the statement. Does the statement remind them of anyone else (such as Gandhi)?

❏ Have students look at the description of the Writing Product. Tell them that as they work through the chapter, they should keep in mind that this will be the major writing assignment for this chapter.

Content Note

King's policy of nonviolent protest was the dominant force in the civil rights movement from 1957 to 1968. King delivered his famous "I Have a Dream" speech at the historic March on Washington in 1963. King was assassinated on April 4, 1968. In 1969, his widow, Coretta Scott King, organized the Martin Luther King, Jr. Center for Non-Violent Social Change.

❝ We must learn to live together as brothers or perish together as fools. ❞

—Martin Luther King, Jr.
American civil rights movement leader, clergyman,
and Nobel Peace Prize winner (1929–1968)

Chapter Overview

Writing Product

An informal letter to a friend

Writing Process

- Describe places to see and things to do in your community.

- Organize paragraphs in a letter.

- Use a graphic organizer to write directions.

- Choose the correct verb tense: simple present and *be going to* for future.

- Use prepositions of location, direction, and distance.

- Use *there*, *it*, and *they.*

- Address an envelope.

Part 1: Before You Write

Exploring Ideas

Building Vocabulary

Organizing Ideas

Using Graphic Organizers

Part 2: Developing Writing Skills

Choosing the Correct Verb Tense

Using Prepositions

Using *There*

Using *It* and *They*

Part 3: Revising and Editing

Revising for Content

Editing for Form

Addressing an Envelope

Evaluating Your Writing

Peer Sharing

Writing the Second Draft

What Do You Think?

Part 4: Expansion Activities

Writing and Researching

Journal Writing

Self-Assessment Log

Exploring Ideas

- ❏ Have students look at the photos. Tell them they are going to discuss the photos in small groups.

1 Describing Places to See and Things to Do

- ❏ Note the group icon. In small groups, have students use the three questions to discuss the photos.

- ❏ After students have finished, have them share their responses with the class.

- ❏ Discuss some of the different types of communities that people live in (e.g., urban, suburban, and rural). Ask students what are the major differences between these types of communities. Ask them what kind of community they would most like to live in.

2 Free Writing

- ❏ Before students write, describe the community in which you live. Model how to use the expressions *there is* and *there are*.

- ❏ Tell students to think about what information might be interesting to people who have never visited their community.

Building Vocabulary

Best Practice

Organizing Information

Throughout this book, students will learn to use a variety of graphic organizers to put their thoughts and ideas together before writing. Completing the following vocabulary chart helps students organize information and vocabulary about their communities into clear and meaningful chunks.

3 Brainstorming Vocabulary

- ❏ Have students look at the vocabulary chart in their books. Ask them how the vocabulary is organized. Point out that listing words by categories or topics can be an effective way to learn new vocabulary.

- ❏ Allow students time to add words to their charts. You might have students return to their groups from Activity 1 for this activity.

- ❏ After students have finished, have several volunteers share their lists with the class. Encourage students to ask questions and comment on these lists.

ANSWER KEY

Answers may vary. Possible answers:

Places to Visit: park, zoo, gardens, library, market, stadium

Things to Do Inside: shop, have a coffee, watch a film

Things to Do Outside: go sightseeing, have a picnic, go to a game

Best Practice

Interacting with Others

Activities such as these give students the opportunity to interact with others and learn from them. In this activity, students share vocabulary lists with a partner and then have a chance to modify their own list. In the following activity, students generate useful new vocabulary through discussion with a partner.

4 Comparing Vocabulary Lists

- ❏ Tell students that this is an opportunity to learn from their partner and modify their own vocabulary list.

5 Generating New Vocabulary Through Discussion

Best Practice

Activating Prior Knowledge

This activity gives students the opportunity to link prior vocabulary knowledge to new vocabulary they acquire through discussion. This expanded vocabulary will be useful to them later, in their writing.

- ❏ Note the pair icon. Review the activity directions and examples with the class.

- ❏ Model or have a volunteer model a sentence using one of the *go* examples.

- ❏ After students have finished, make a list of new *go* vocabulary on the board.

ANSWER KEY

Answers may vary. Possible answers:

go out to dinner, go for a drive, go skydiving, go dancing, go downtown

6 Creating a Map

- ❏ Note the group icon. Have students discuss their experiences with giving and receiving directions. Ask: *What kinds of information are useful (such as landmarks or mileage)? What causes confusion?*

- ❏ Ask students to label each element of their maps and to create a legend, or key, which explains the meaning of their map's symbols. If possible, bring in a map with a legend to show students.

- ❏ Have students practice giving their directions to their partner. Then have them discuss whether the directions were clear and easy to understand.

Organizing Ideas

Briefly review with students what they have already learned about a paragraph.

1. The topic sentence gives the main idea of the paragraph. The topic sentence is often, but not always, the first sentence.

2. Paragraphs usually start with general ideas and progress to more specific ones.

3. The last sentence of a paragraph often describes a personal reaction, opinion, or feeling.

Best Practice

Scaffolding Instruction

This chapter makes extensive use of structured, clear, and authentic activities. The activities systematically build on one another to prepare the student to write a letter inviting a friend to visit. The scaffolding practices employed help students learn to give concise directions, create a map, and effectively organize paragraphs in a letter before constructing their final writing product.

ORGANIZING PARAGRAPHS IN A LETTER

- ■ After the students have had a chance to read silently, read the explanation of the three different paragraphs with the class.

- ■ Ask students why it is important to organize paragraphs in a letter. Elicit that the general information early in a letter gives the reader a context and then the specific information adds detail. It is also important for a letter to have an effective closing.

7 Ordering Ideas in a Letter

- ❏ Have students read the list of sentences and decide if they belong in paragraph 1, 2, or 3. Review the example with the class.

- ❏ After students have finished, review answers with the class. Ask students why each sentence belongs in that paragraph.

ANSWER KEY

a. 1 b. 2 c. 1 d. 2 e. 2 f. 1 g. 1 h. 3

EXPANSION ACTIVITY

- ■ Tell students they are going to think of new ideas to include in the letter.

- ■ Create three columns on the board, labeled *1st Paragraph, 2nd Paragraph,* and *3rd Paragraph.*

- Ask students to think about additional sentences that would fit the model letter you've been discussing. Write an example in each column, such as (1st Paragraph) *My city is a very exciting place to visit*; (2nd Paragraph) *My house is the third on the right*; and (3rd Paragraph) *We're going to have a lot of fun*.

- Ask students to give sentences of their own and state which paragraph they belong in, and why.

- Write some examples on the board.

Using Graphic Organizers

❑ Students will use a graphic organizer to order the information they give in directions.

Strategy

Giving Directions

Ask students if someone has ever given them directions—but not in a clear, ordered way. Give an example, such as: *You drive down Main Street, then turn left at the light. At the next light, turn right. Oh, and on Main Street, there will be a bank on the left before you turn.*

8 Analyzing a Graphic Organizer

❑ Review activity directions with students.

❑ Have volunteers read the directions and "other information" aloud.

❑ Make sure to elicit any unnecessary information from the students, such as: *My father's office is on this street*.

❑ Are the directions presented in a clear and ordered way?

- Ask students to create a very basic map based on the directions in Activity 8.

- Have students refer to Activity 6 as a model.

- Ask for volunteers to present their maps on the board.

9 Creating a Graphic Organizer

❑ Note the pair icon. After students have finished, have them work with a partner to assess the effectiveness of their directions.

❑ If they feel any directions are unclear or out of order, have them brainstorm additional ways to give or order the directions. Do the directions work seamlessly with the map?

❑ Ask students to volunteer any valuable lessons or techniques they learned in the activity.

Developing Cohesion and Clarity

CHOOSING THE CORRECT VERB TENSE

- Review the verb tense chart with the class. Point out that the future with *be going to* uses the present continuous tense of *be*: *We are going to the beach tomorrow*. Also point out that a contraction is often used: *We're going*, rather than *We are going*.

- Ask students to create sentences using these two tenses, such as: *I'm in class right now. I'm going to visit my grandmother after school*.

1 Adding the Correct Verb to Sentences

Best Practice

Cultivating Critical Thinking

Activities such as these teach a particular critical thinking skill and provide varied opportunities for practicing it. In this case, students are asked to choose the correct verb tense to complete a paragraph. In the following activities, students are asked to identify prepositions, add them to sentences, and use them to effectively give directions. They also must correctly complete sentences with *there* and *it*. The expansion activities after Activity 4 and Activity 6 provide more opportunity for synthesizing and applying this skill.

- Review the activity directions and example.

- After students have finished, review answers with the class.

ANSWER KEY
Answers may vary. Possible answers:

1. are 2. 're/are going to have 3. 's/is, 's/is going to be hot 4. 's/is 5. know 6. is going to give, is giving 7. is going to have, is having 8. going to be 9. go

USING PREPOSITIONS

- Review the information about using prepositions with the class.

- Elicit additional examples of place, direction, and distance from the students: The football field is <u>behind</u> the school. Turn left <u>onto</u> Highway 111. Drive <u>for</u> six miles.

2 Identifying Prepositions

- Review the activity directions and first example.

- After students have finished, review answers with the class.

ANSWER KEY

Take Route 44 south (to) Exit 12. Turn right (at) the first light. You will be (on) Maple Avenue. Go straight (down) Maple Avenue (for) two miles. (At) the corner of Bryant and Maple, you will see an elementary school. Turn right (at) the first street (after) the school. The name of the street is Roosevelt Drive. Go straight (for) five blocks. Then make a left turn (onto) Broadmoor. My apartment building isn't difficult to find. It's (on) the left, number 122. You can park your car (behind) the building.

3 Adding Prepositions to Sentences

- Review the activity directions and first example. Ask students if there are any other possible answers for the first example: *on*.

- After students have finished, review possible answers with the class.

ANSWER KEY

1. at/on 2. to 3. at 4. on 5. for 6. at 7. on

4 **Using Prepositions to Give Directions**

Best Practice

Interacting with Others

Activities such as this give students the opportunity to interact with a partner and receive constructive feedback on their directions. Students can clearly gauge the effectiveness of their directions by whether their partner is successful in reaching the destination. The expansion activity that follows gives students the opportunity to apply what they've learned to a real-life situation.

❑ You might begin the activity by giving directions to a student as a model. Ask students if the directions were clear.

❑ Discuss students' experiences with directions. Do they prefer written or oral directions? Why? Do they prefer using a map or asking a person for directions?

❑ This activity can be done as a written or an oral exercise. In either case, the student giving the directions should not reveal the destination until and unless the other student reaches it.

REPRODUCIBLE   EXPANSION ACTIVITY

■ Photocopy and distribute **Black Line Master 8**, "How to Get to My Home," on page BLM8 of this Teacher's Edition.

■ Tell students that they are going to work in pairs and give each other directions for how to get to where they each live from school.

■ Go over the directions with the class, and ask if students have any questions.

USING *THERE, IT,* AND *THEY*

■ Review Using *There* and Using *It* and *They* with the class.

■ Elicit additional examples of *there* to introduce a subject: *There isn't a good restaurant in this neighborhood*.

■ Elicit additional examples of *there* referring to a specific place: *My uncle lives in Berlin. I don't go there very often*.

■ Elicit additional examples of *it* to describe the weather or a situation: *It's sunny and hot today*.

■ Elicit additional examples of *it* and *they* used as pronouns: *The capital of my country is Amman. It's a beautiful city. My family worries about me. They're always calling*.

5 **Analyzing the Use of *There* and *It***

❑ Review the activity directions and first example.

❑ After students have finished, ask students to write sentences on the board, circling and underlining the appropriate words. Discuss and correct each example as a class.

ANSWER KEY

1. There is a supermarket on the corner. (It) has a big red and white sign. 2. The museum is very interesting. I like to go (there). 3. We can't have a picnic. It's rainy today. 4. I like New York City. There is a beautiful park (there). 5. It is difficult to find housing in New York City.

6 **Completing Sentences with *There* and *It***

❑ Review the activity directions and the first example.

❑ After students have finished, ask volunteers to share their answers with the class.

❑ When appropriate, ask students what *there* or *it* refers to.

ANSWER KEY

1. There (introduces a subject)

2. It (refers to a specific place, Washington, D.C.)

3. there (refers to Washington, D.C.)

4. there (says that something exists in a specific location)

5. it (refers to a specific place, the "large open area")

6. There (introduces a subject)

7. there (refers to a place, the mall)

8. There (refers to something that exists in a certain location)

9. It (a pronoun, referring to "a very large, famous structure")

Best Practice

Making Use of Academic Content

The following expansion activity contains real-world, authentic material that gives students experience in using prepositions and *there* and *it* to give directions. This application of the content they have just learned will help them internalize and become more confident with the material.

EXPANSION ACTIVITY

- Tell students that they are going to play a game where they give their classmates directions to locations in the neighborhood.

- Model an example by giving students oral directions to a location near your school. Start at your current location. Use prepositions, *there* and *it* as much as possible. When you are finished ask, *Where are we?*

- Have volunteers follow your example.

- Monitor students' directions and give constructive feedback where appropriate.

7 **Writing the First Draft**

- ❑ Have students write their first drafts of a letter inviting a friend to visit.

- ❑ Remind them to use their community vocabulary and ideas from Part 1, Activity 3, use future with *be going to* to tell what is going to happen, use prepositions to give clear and accurate directions, and use *there* and *it* where appropriate.

- ❑ Emphasize that a first draft is a very rough form of writing. Students should write complete, logical sentences and paragraphs, but they will revise these later. The content is the most important factor in the rough draft.

Revising for Content and Editing for Form

1 Revising for Content

- ❑ Review the activity directions with the class.

- ❑ Remind students that this is a revision for content and organization and they shouldn't be concerned with detail. They are only identifying paragraphs here.

- ❑ After students have finished, review possible changes with the class. For this activity, focus *only* on the division of the letter into paragraphs. Students will edit the same letter for form in the next activity, after they have reviewed a sample informal letter and writing guidelines.

SAMPLE LETTER

June 15, 2006
Dear Moustapha,

I'm very glad that you visit me next week. We will to have a good time.

It's easy to find my house. Make left turn at the corner of Broadway and Fifth Street. Drive down Fifth two blocks. Make a right turn on Henry Street. There are a park on the corner. My house is on the left side. It are number 150.

the weather is warm so we can going hiking and swimming. Please to bring your photo album. I want see the pictures of your family.

EDITING FOR FORM: USING CORRECT FORM IN AN INFORMAL LETTER

- ■ Review the sample informal letter and writing guidelines with the class.

- ■ Ask students if they can describe any differences between an informal letter and a formal letter. Who would they send an informal letter to? A formal letter?

2 Editing for Form

- ❑ Review the activity directions with the class.

- ❑ Remind students to focus on form: correct use of future with *be going to*, using prepositions to give directions, using *there*, using *it* and *they*, and other "micro" issues. You might want to review some of this with students before they edit.

- ❑ After students have finished, have several students share the changes they made with the class. Write a model on the board.

SAMPLE LETTER

June 15, 2006

Dear Moustapha,

I'm very glad that you are going to visit me next week. We will have such a good time.

It's easy to find my house. Make a left turn at the corner of Broadway and Fifth Street. Drive down Fifth for two blocks. Then make a right turn on Henry Street. There is a park on the corner. My house is on the left side. It is number 150.

The weather is warm, so we can go hiking and swimming. Please bring your photo album. I want see to the pictures of your family.

See you soon.

Yours,

Michael

ADDRESSING AN ENVELOPE

- ■ Review the sample envelope and writing guidelines with the class.

- ■ Ask students if envelopes are addressed the same way in their countries. Have them explain what differences there are, if any.

- Ask students how much it costs to mail a letter or postcard in their countries. Is it more or less expensive than here?

---

3 Addressing an Envelope

- ❏ Review the activity directions with the class.
- ❏ Go over capitalization rules, state abbreviations, and ZIP codes with the class.
- ❏ Have a volunteer address the letter in a rectangle drawn on the board and allow other students to comment.

ANSWER KEY

Answers may vary. Possible answers:

Michael Ryall
150 Henry Street
Monterey, CA 93940

Mary Pirewali
256 Rose Avenue
San Jose, CA
95101

Evaluating Your Writing

4 Using a Rubric

Best Practice

Cultivating Critical Thinking

Activities such as these require students to critically evaluate their own and others' letter writing based on both set criteria and more general guidelines. Students then make judgments and suggestions on the overall quality of the letters.

- ❏ Review the rubric with your class. Using the sample informal letter to Bill on page 69 of the Student Book, ask volunteers to evaluate it based on the first criteria: **Content** – *Letter includes salutation, clear directions, information*

about places to see and/or things to do, and a closing.

- ❏ Then have students use the rubric to score the letter they wrote to a friend.

Writing with Computers

- After the students have had a chance to read silently, read the text aloud or ask a volunteer to read it aloud.
- Do students agree with the advice about working with a hard copy?

5 Peer Sharing

Best Practice

Interacting with Others

Activities such as this give students the opportunity to interact with a partner and receive constructive feedback on their letter writing. Here, students share their letters with a partner who evaluates it according to his or her own understanding of good writing practices. Students also get to see how their work is similar to and different from their peers' work.

- ❏ Note the pair icon. Give students time to exchange letters and read each other's work.
- ❏ Students should compare their letters and discuss how they are similar or different.
- ❏ Have a volunteer pair of students share their results with the class.

6 Writing the Second Draft

- ❏ Have students rewrite their letters based on their own rubric evaluation from Activity 4 and what they've learned in this chapter.
- ❏ Collect student letters and make comments and corrections.
- ❏ Return students' letters; then circulate through the classroom, discussing students' work and your feedback.

7 **Evaluating Your Progress**

Best Practice

Cultivating Critical Thinking

Activities such as this one require students to try to objectively analyze how they are progressing with their writing. By answering the questions and writing in their journals, students are forced to think about their own strengths and weaknesses.

❑ Review the activity directions with the class.

❑ To instill confidence in students, you might walk around the class during this activity, briefly discussing with each student some of their strengths and what areas need improvement.

❑ More extensive counseling can be conducted individually.

What Do You Think?

Evaluating Your Community's Services

■ Review the activity directions with the class.

■ This activity could utilize the Internet, local newspapers, or other relevant materials. You can give students assistance in identifying local websites, such as Yahoo—Get Local™.

■ Divide students into small groups to answer the questions; then discuss their answers as a class.

■ A possible follow-up activity might be to have students prepare small brochures on the activities available at your school or in your community.

Best Practice

Organizing Information

The expansion activity that follows uses a graphic organizer—a cluster/word web—that helps students organize information in a logical and visual way.

 REPRODUCIBLE **EXPANSION ACTIVITY**

■ Photocopy and distribute **Black Line Master 9**, "Mapping Information," on page BLM9 of this Teacher's Edition.

■ Tell students that they are going to use a graphic organizer—a cluster/word web—to map information about the types of activities that are available at their school and in their communities.

■ Go over the directions with the class and answer any questions students may have.

■ Ask volunteers to suggest how to fill in the first few circles.

Best Practice

Best Practice

Making Use of Academic Content

This section of the chapter contains content-based, authentic activities that give students experience in getting directions, writing and responding to informal letters, and researching a city or town.

1 Getting Directions

- ❏ Note the pair icon. Have students draw simple maps based on their partner's directions. The person who gave directions can check the map to make sure the directions are well-written and easy to understand. Students can then write responses to the invitations.

- ❏ You might model a simple map on the board using directions to your house. You might also model a brief, generic reply to an invitation to visit someone in order to help the students get started.

- ❏ This activity might need to be continued outside the classroom as homework.

- ❏ Have the students discuss what is most important in giving good directions.

2 Inviting a Classmate to Your House

- ❏ Have students write an informal letter to a classmate. Refer them to the letter on page 69 of the Student Book as a model for the format.

- ❏ Tell students that they can reuse the map they drew for BLM 9 here.

3 Writing in Your Journal

- ❏ If students seem to have difficulty with either activity, suggest that they generate their own ideas for journal topics that are related to the theme of the chapter.

4 Researching a City or Town

- ❏ Review the activity directions with the class.

- ❏ Ideally this activity should be done using the Internet. If Internet access is not available to the students, you can provide tourist brochures or other reference materials appropriate to the task.

- ❏ Ask students to share some of what they learned with the class.

Self-Assessment Log

- ❏ Review the statements in the self-assessment log and then have students complete it.

5

Home

Chapter Opener

- ❑ Point out the title of this chapter, "Home." Ask students what comes to mind when they think about the title and to make predictions about what this chapter's theme is likely to be.

- ❑ Have students look at the photo. Ask students whether they find this home unusual, and why. Ask and answer the questions in Connecting to the Topic.

- ❑ Read the quotation or call on a student to read it. Share some of the content information about Lois McMaster Bujold with students. Then ask them if they agree or disagree with the statement. Ask students what most represents "home" for them.

- ❑ Have students look at the description of the Writing Product. Tell them that as they work through the chapter, they should keep in mind that this will be the major writing assignment for this chapter.

Content Note

Bujold is an award-winning science fiction and fantasy writer who has published 16 novels to date. She is best known for her stories set approximately 1,000 years in the future about the Vorkosigan family from the planet Barrayar. Her hero, Miles Vorkosigan, is a military genius with bones of glass. She has won an unprecedented four Hugo Awards for her works in the *Vorkosigan Saga*. A mother of two, Bujold lives in Minneapolis, Minnesota.

❝ My home is not a place, it is a people. ❞

—Lois McMaster Bujold
American writer (1949–)

Chapter Overview

Writing Product

A narrative paragraph about a part of your life

Writing Process

- Use a timeline to organize information in chronological order.

- Write a topic sentence for a narrative paragraph.

- Learn to limit information in a narrative paragraph.

- Learn to punctuate titles.

- Use the past tense to talk about your life.

- Combine sentences with time words and *because*.

- Punctuate sentences with dependent clauses.

Part 1: Before You Write

Exploring Ideas

Building Vocabulary

Organizing Ideas

Writing Topic Sentences

Part 2: Developing Writing Skills

Combining Sentences with Time Words and *Because*

Punctuating Sentences with Dependent Clauses

Writing the First Draft

Part 3: Revising and Editing

Revising for Content

Editing for Form

Evaluating Your Writing

Peer Sharing

Writing the Second Draft

What do You Think?

Part 4: Expansion Activities

Writing and Researching

Journal Writing

Self-Assessment Log

Exploring Ideas

EXPANSION ACTIVITY

- Have students work in small groups. Ask students to think of other examples of unconventional homes or lifestyles (such as recreational vehicles or nomadic tribes).

- Have the groups discuss whether they can imagine living in that kind of situation. What would be the challenges? What might be the benefits? Is there one best way to live?

- After the discussion, have each group share their ideas with the class.

❏ Call on a volunteer to read the information in the strategy box at the top of page 78 in their Student Books.

❏ Ask students to give examples of some important times in their lives (such as first job and first overseas trip).

Best Practice

Making Use of Academic Content

Activities such as these contain authentic material that gives students the opportunity to discuss real-world experiences. Students use information about their own lives and the lives of other students to create and write about lifelines, as well as to generate new vocabulary through discussion. This application of real-life content will help them internalize and become more confident with the writing process.

1   Creating a Lifeline

❏ To get students started, it may be helpful if you model how to do this activity on the board. Draw a timeline as described in the Student Book. Then write a few important events and turning points in your life and your corresponding feelings.

❏ After the students have finished, invite volunteers to write their lifelines on the board.

Building Vocabulary

2   Generating Vocabulary Through Discussion

Best Practice

Activating Prior Knowledge

This activity gives students the opportunity to link prior knowledge of vocabulary related to life experiences to new vocabulary they acquire through discussion with their group. This expanded vocabulary will be useful to them later in their writing.

❏ Note the group icon. Encourage students to ask as many questions about each others' lifelines as they can.

❏ After students have finished, ask students to give examples of some of the new vocabulary they learned during this activity. Write some examples on the board.

Organizing Ideas

Strategy

Limiting Information

- Review the strategy for limiting information with the class.

- Ask students to think of a period on their lifelines that would be interesting to others.

Best Practice

Scaffolding Instruction

The activities in this chapter systematically build on one another in order to prepare the student to write a narrative paragraph about a period in his or her life. These scaffolding practices help students learn to choose the best topic, write a topic sentence, write a title, use the past tense, use time words, conjunctions, and *because*, and to punctuate sentences with dependent clauses.

3 Choosing the Best Topic

- ❑ Note the group icon. Have the students discuss what they find most interesting or unusual about the woman's timeline.

- ❑ Remind students that a paragraph is typically organized around related information.

- ❑ After the students have finished, ask the different groups what they chose as the most interesting part of this woman's life.

4 Defining Your Topic

- ❑ Make sure that students understand that the activity is asking them to focus on one period of their lives. They can use the questions to help them evaluate and refine their choice of topic.

Best Practice

Organizing Information

The expansion activity that follows uses a graphic organizer to help students organize information about their lives in a logical and visual way in preparation for writing a narrative paragraph.

 EXPANSION ACTIVITY

- ◼ Tell students that they are going to use a graphic organizer to help them organize information for their paragraphs.

- ◼ Photocopy and distribute **Black Line Master 10,** "My Life," on page BLM10 of this Teacher's Edition, and go over the directions with the class. Tell them that they will write the topic of their paragraph in the Topic box and add information about events in that period of their lives that are interesting. Have them write down why those events might be interesting to someone else.

- ◼ Have the students, in pairs, exchange organizers and discuss what they have written.

5 Discussing Your Topic

- ❑ Note the pair icon. Encourage students to give each other feedback on their choices.

- ❑ Tell students that they may choose a different period to write about if their discussion leads them to believe it is better to do so.

- ❑ After the students have finished, ask volunteers to tell which period of their lives they chose and explain why.

6 Brainstorming Ideas

- ❑ You might walk around the class during this activity, briefly discussing with each student some of his or her ideas.

- ❑ Remind students that they are writing one paragraph and all the ideas that they circle should be related.

Writing Topic Sentences

- ❑ Ask students to think about what they've already learned about topic sentences.

- ❑ Invite a volunteer to give a definition of a topic sentence: a topic sentence gives the main idea of the paragraph, is always a complete sentence with a subject and a verb, and is often, but not always, the first sentence in a paragraph.

7 Choosing the Best Topic Sentence

- ❑ Review the activity directions with the class. After the students have finished, ask for volunteers to answer and explain why they chose that sentence.

ANSWER KEY

Paragraph 1: 1 Paragraph 2: 3

8 **Writing a Draft Topic Sentence**

- ❑ Note the pair icon. After the students have finished writing their two possible topic sentences, have them find a partner.

- ❑ You might walk around the class during this activity, briefly discussing with each pair of students their choices. Was the pair in agreement on the final choices? If not, help them to work through their differences.

Strategy

Writing a Title

- ■ Review the information about writing a title with the class.

- ■ Have students give examples of great book and movie titles and write some examples on the board. These can serve as models for students' paragraph titles.

9 **Correcting Titles**

- ❑ Remind students to use the guidelines in the Writing a Title strategy.

ANSWER KEY

1. An Exciting Life 2. All's Well That Ends Well
3. A Gift of Hope 4. The Best Years of My Life
5. Going Away 6. A Happy Ending 7. Life in a New City 8. Best Friends 9. A New Beginning
10. A Wonderful Experience

10 **Choosing the Best Titles**

- ❑ Tell students that there might be more than one correct choice.

- ❑ After students have had time to choose, ask for volunteers to explain their choices.

- ❑ Have students vote, by show of hands, for their favorite title for each paragraph.

ANSWER KEY

Answers may vary. Possible answers:

Paragraph 1: Born a Twin, My Childhood as a Twin

Paragraph 2: Unhappy Teens, Teenage Years

11 **Writing Draft Titles**

- ❑ Note the pair icon. Allow students time to have brief writing conferences with a partner to share and evaluate their writing titles.

- ❑ Ask volunteers to share their draft titles with the class. Do other students think the titles are interesting?

Developing Cohesion and Clarity

1 Using the Past Tense

Best Practice

Critical Thinking

Activities such as these teach important critical thinking skills and provide varied opportunities for practicing them. In this case, students are asked to use the correct past tense form of different verbs to complete a paragraph. In the following activities, students are asked to write sentences with past tense verbs, correctly punctuate sentences with dependent clauses, write sentences with time words, conjunctions, and *because*, and use all of these skills to write a first draft of a narrative paragraph. The expansion activity after Activity 5 provides more opportunity for synthesizing and applying these skills.

❑ Review the activity directions. Complete the first sentence with the class.

❑ Remind students that verbs can be both regular (*-ed*) and irregular in the past tense.

❑ After students have finished, review answers with the class.

ANSWER KEY

1. was 2. had 3. was 4. had 5. fed 6. played
7. cried 8. did 9. needed 10. wanted 11. was
not/wasn't 12. was 13. worked 14. complained

2 Writing Sentences with Past Tense Verbs

❑ Remind students that they can't use past tense verbs for things they are still doing.

❑ Encourage students to check each others' work for variation in verb choice and correct tense.

❑ After students have finished, ask volunteers to share some of their sentences. Write examples on the board. Is it a regular or an irregular verb?

COMBINING SENTENCES WITH TIME WORDS AND *BECAUSE*

■ Review the information and examples with the class.

■ Remind students that they can review how to combine sentences with *and*, *but*, or *so* in Chapter 1, and elicit at least one example of each from the class: *I lived in Cairo* and *Amman. My mother is from Spain*, but *my father is from Morocco. My father was in the military*, so *we moved a lot*. Write one example of each on the board.

■ Point out to students that, with time words and *because,* the two parts of the sentence (clauses) can usually be reversed with no change in meaning: *Before I started school, I was very happy. = I was very happy before I started school.*

3 Completing Sentences with Time Words, Conjunctions, and *Because*

❑ Review the activity directions and first example.

❑ After students have finished, review answers with the class.

ANSWER KEY

1. before 2. when 3. Before 4. as soon as/after
5. and 6. Because 7. so 8. and 9. When

4 Completing Sentences with Information from Your Life

❑ Review the activity directions and first example.

❑ You might begin the activity by giving a few personal examples: *I decided to teach English* because *I love to help people. After I left high school, I traveled in Europe for six months.*

❑ After students have finished, ask volunteers to share some of their sentences. Write some examples on the board. Is the verb regular or irregular? Can the clauses be reversed with no change in meaning?

ANSWER KEY

Answers may vary. Possible answers:

1. When I became a teenager, I had a strong desire to travel. 2. I decided to study English because I wanted to be an airline pilot. 3. When I was a child, I was always getting into trouble. 4. After I left high school, I immediately got a job. 5. Before I started this class, I never practiced my English.

PUNCTUATING SENTENCES WITH DEPENDENT CLAUSES

- Review the information and examples with the class.

- Have students give additional examples of sentences that can have the dependent clause at the beginning or end of the sentence with no change in meaning (such as, *After I got my first job, I bought a car.* = *I bought a car after I got my first job.*). Ask volunteers to write their two sentences on the board. Review the correct use of commas.

---

5 **Combining Sentences**

- ❑ Review the activity directions and first example.

- ❑ After students have finished, ask volunteers to write the combined sentences on the board. Discuss each example and alternative answers as a class.

- ❑ Discuss the change in meaning with sentence 5 when the clauses are reversed.

ANSWER KEY

Answers may vary. Possible answers:

1. Because I was a good student, I got a scholarship./I got a scholarship because I was a good student. 2. I graduated from high school

when I was 16./When I was 16, I graduated from high school. 3. After my father died, my mother went to work./My mother went to work after my father died. 4. I found a job as soon as I finished high school./As soon as I finished high school, I found a job. 5. I stopped studying, so I was unhappy./I was unhappy, so I stopped studying.

REPRODUCIBLE **EXPANSION ACTIVITY**

- ■ Photocopy and distribute **Black Line Master 11**,"In the Past," on page BLM11 of this Teacher's Edition.

- ■ Tell students that they are going to combine sentences with time words, conjunctions, and *because*. They will be writing multiple answers for each example.

- ■ Go over the directions and first example with the class, and ask if students have any questions.

- ■ After students have finished, discuss all possible answers for each example. Do any of the alternatives have different meanings?

6 **Writing Sentences with Time Words and *Because***

- ❑ Review the activity directions and first example. Instruct students to write their own example with *before*, and call on volunteers to share their answers.

- ❑ After students have finished the activity, ask volunteers to share their answers with the class. Write some examples on the board.

- ❑ When appropriate, ask students to give alternative versions of the sentence.

ANSWER KEY

Answers may vary. Possible answers:

1. Before I started school, I taught myself to read.
2. I never had a lot of friends because we moved so much. 3. After my mother died, my father remarried. 4. When I was 13, I got a dog. 5. I got my own apartment as soon as I graduated from high school.

7 Writing the First Draft

❑ Review the elements students need to include when they write their first drafts of a paragraph about an important time in their lives.

❑ Emphasize that a first draft is a rough form of writing. Students should write a complete, logical paragraph using time words and *because*, but they will revise this later. The content is the most important factor in the rough draft.

Revising for Content and Editing for Form

1 Revising for Content

- ❏ Remind students that this is a revision for content and organization where they are focusing on combining sentences with the conjunctions *and*, *but*, and *so*. They will further edit the paragraph for form in Activity 3.

- ❏ After students have finished, review possible changes with the class.

- ❏ **Note to Instructor:** The following sample paragraph has been revised for both content and form and should be referred to for both Activities 1 and 3.

SAMPLE PARAGRAPH

How I Became a Jazz Musician

I fell in love with jazz when I was five years old. I always heard jazz in the streets, but for my fifth birthday my brother took me to a concert. That was the first time I saw a great saxophonist, and I decided to learn to play the saxophone. First I needed a saxophone, so I asked my father. My father said he had no money for a saxophone, so I worked for my brother, uncles, and cousins. I made a little money and my father saw that I was working hard, so he gave me money for a saxophone. I listened to recordings and my brother taught me. I practiced every day, and soon I was a good saxophone player.

2 Editing Practice: Independent and Dependent Clauses

- ❏ Review the activity directions and first example with the class.

- ❏ Remind students that dependent clauses (sentence fragments) cannot stand alone and are followed by a comma when they appear at the beginning of a sentence.

- ❏ After students have finished, review answers with the class.

ANSWER KEY

1. Before we moved here, we used to have many friends and relatives nearby. 2. Correct 3. Correct. 4. We moved to Colorado because the doctors said I needed a dry climate. 5. When I first came here, I loved the excitement of New York. 6. I came to the city when I was five.

EXPANSION ACTIVITY

- ■ Tell students that they are going to write additional sentences about their pasts. Each sentence should contain both an independent and dependent clause.

- ■ Have students use time words, conjunctions, and *because* to write past tense sentences about their lives. Tell students to pay attention to punctuation.

- ■ Have students share some of their sentences with the class and write examples on the board. Is there a comma in the sentence? Where does it go? What is the independent and dependent clause?

3 Editing for Form

- ❏ Review the activity directions with the class.

- ❏ After students have finished, review possible changes with the class.

- ❏ **Note to Instructor:** The sample paragraph following Activity 1 has been revised for both content and form and should be referred to for both Activities 1 and 3.

Evaluating Your Writing

4 Using a Rubric

> **Best Practice**
>
> **Cultivating Critical Thinking**
>
> Activities such as these require students to critically evaluate their own and others' writing based on both specific criteria and more general guidelines. In this and the following activity, students rate their own narrative paragraph and then conference with a partner to make judgments and suggestions about the overall quality of the paragraphs.

❑ Review the rubric with your class. Using the completed sample paragraph about the twins on Student Book pages 82–83 and one of the titles chosen to go with it, ask volunteers to evaluate it based on the first criteria: *Content – Paragraph presents information about a specific period in the writer's life.*

❑ Then have students use the rubric to evaluate the paragraph they wrote.

5 Peer Sharing

> **Best Practice**
>
> **Interacting with Others**
>
> Activities such as this give students the opportunity to interact with a partner and receive constructive feedback on their writing. Here, students share their narrative paragraphs with a partner, who evaluates it according to his or her own understanding of good writing practices. Students also get to see how their work is similar to and different from their peers' work.

❑ Note the pair icon. Give students time to exchange paragraphs and read each other's work.

❑ Students should discuss how interesting the paragraphs are and if they'd like to read more about that person's life.

❑ Have volunteer pairs of students share their results with the class.

6 Writing the Second Draft

❑ Have students rewrite their paragraphs based on their own rubric evaluation from Activity 4 and what they've learned in this chapter.

❑ Collect student paragraphs and make comments and corrections.

❑ Return students' paragraphs, then circulate through the classroom, discussing students' work and your feedback.

Writing with Computers

- Review the information about saving drafts with the class.

- Do students agree with the advice about saving drafts? Have they ever lost work on the computer? Ask students if they think writing can ever be revised too much. Do they think it's possible for a first draft to be final?

What Do You think?

Birth Order

- Review the birth order information with the class.

- Discuss this theory with your class and ask students to give examples from their own lives either supporting or arguing against the theory.

- Have students use the questions in Thinking About Your Birth Order as a stimulus for writing in their journals.

Best Practice

Making Use of Academic Content

This section of the chapter contains content-based, authentic activities that give students experience in using realia to enrich their stories, interviewing and writing about a friend's life experiences, practice in writing fantasy, and writing about the happiest or saddest time in their lives.

1 Sharing Your Writing

- ❑ This activity will need to be prepared outside the classroom as homework.

- ❑ Note the group icon. Have students use the photographs, their paragraphs, and anything else they can think of to describe the period in their lives that they wrote about.

- ❑ You might model this activity by showing some pictures of your own and verbally describing that period of time in your life.

- ❑ Have the students discuss how to evaluate narrative writing. Does the writing involve the reader in the story? Are there universal aspects to the writer's story that other people will be able to relate to? Are details given to support and enhance the story?

EXPANSION ACTIVITY

- Tell students that they are going to do an activity very similar to Activity 1, but about someone else in their family (such as a parent or grandparent).

- Have the students find photographs of a period of time in that person's life and write a paragraph about it. This could be especially interesting if it involves an oral history passed down by a grandparent.

- Have the students share their photographs and paragraphs with the class.

2 Interviewing a Friend

- ❏ Note the pair icon. Have students write a narrative paragraph based on an interview with a friend, relative, or other interesting person. This activity can be done in class or as homework.

- ❏ Tell students to use everything they've learned in this chapter to maximize the impact of their paragraph on the reader.

3 Writing from the Imagination

- ❏ Review the activity directions and example with the class.

- ❏ If students seem to have difficulty with the writing activity, ask them to describe the life of a character from a book or movie that they admired using the past tense.

4 Writing in Your Journal

- ❏ The topics in the Student Book can be used as prompts for journal writing, but students should be encouraged to generate their own ideas, such as *The most exciting time in my life*; *The worst time in my life*.

5 Researching a Famous Person in History

- ❏ Ideally this activity should be done using the Internet. If Internet access is not available to the students, have them use the library, or you can provide encyclopedias or other reference books (such as the *Who's Who?* series of books).

- ❏ Ask students to share their paragraphs with the class.

Self-Assessment Log

- ❏ Review the statements in the self-assessment log and then have students complete it.

6

Cultures of the World

Chapter Opener

❏ Point out the title of this chapter, "Cultures of the World." Ask students to discuss the meaning of *culture* and to make predictions about what this chapter's theme is likely to be.

❏ Have students look at the photo. Explain that this is a picture of a storyteller who is telling a folktale to children. Ask students to discuss what a folktale is. Ask and answer the questions in Connecting to the Topic.

❏ Read the quotation or call on a student to read it. Share some of the content information about Isaac Bashevis Singer with the students. Then ask them if they agree or disagree with the statement. What does the verb *redeem* mean? Ask students what makes a story interesting for them.

❏ Have students look at the description of the Writing Product. Tell them that as they work through the chapter, they should keep in mind that this will be the major writing assignment for this chapter.

Content Note

Born Icek-Hersz Zynger in a town near Warsaw, Poland, Isaac Bashevis Singer was a journalist, novelist, short-story writer, and essayist. He is best known for his stories of traditional Polish life. Singer won the Nobel Prize in Literature in 1978. He became an American citizen in 1943 and was elected to the National Institute of Arts and Letters in 1964.

❝ A good writer is basically a story-teller, not a scholar or a redeemer of mankind. ❞

—Isaac Bashevis Singer
Polish-born American writer (1904–1991)

Chapter Overview

Writing Product

A one-paragraph story ending

Writing Process

- Read and discuss a folktale.

- Learn about story elements.

- Use a plot diagram.

- Use time words to describe a sequence of events.

- Limit information in a narrative paragraph.

- Use time words to write about events in the past.

- Use editing symbols.

Part 1: Before You Write

Exploring Ideas

Building Vocabulary

Organizing Ideas

Using Graphic Organizers

Part 2: Developing Writing Skills

Writing About Two Events That Occurred in the Past

Using *As Soon As*

Using *Then*

Writing the First Draft

Part 3: Revising and Editing

Revising for Content

Editing for Form

Evaluating Your Writing

Peer Sharing

Writing the Second Draft

Foucs on Testing

What Do You Think?

Part 4: Expansion Activities

Writing and Researching

Journal Writing

Self-Assessment Log

What Do You Think?

Exploring Ideas

EXPANSION ACTIVITY

- ■ Tell students that myths, folktales, and fairy tales are often part of a culture's oral tradition. As a class, discuss what an oral tradition is and its importance to culture.

- ■ Have students work in small groups. Have each group choose one myth, folktale, or fairy tale to discuss. If students have problems thinking of a tale, ask a volunteer in the group to tell the others a myth, folktale, or fairy tale from his or her home country.

- ■ Have students discuss these questions: *What is the message or meaning of the story? Does the story have any relevance to our world today?*

- ■ Have each group report back to the class on the story they chose. Allow students to comment and ask questions.

- ❑ Review the information on folktales with the class.

- ❑ Ask students to talk about how they learned folktales when they were children and what significance the tales had for them.

Best Practice

Making Use of Academic Content

Activities such as these contain authentic material that can lead to discussion of real issues in students' lives. Here, students use a German folktale to generate new vocabulary, brainstorm different endings to the story, use plot diagrams to learn about story elements, and write good titles. This application of content will help them prepare for the writing task ahead.

1 Reading a Folktale

- ❑ Model pronunciation and intonation by reading the folktale aloud. Then invite volunteers to take turns reading parts of the folktale aloud for the class.

- ❑ Check comprehension by asking students to retell the folktale in their own words.

- ❑ Point out that the folktale is incomplete as presented here. The ending will be revealed later in the chapter.

Building Vocabulary

2 Identifying Vocabulary Words

- ❑ Review the activity directions and first example.

- ❑ After students have finished, review answers with the class. Ask students, for each word they found, to identify the part of speech it is (For example, *hut* is a noun).

ANSWER KEY

1. a small house: hut (noun) 2. a large container; a bushel (noun) 3. selfish: greedy (adjective) 4. a person who digs for coal: miner (noun) 5. unselfish: generous (adjective) 6. a kind of meat: beef (noun) 7. the home of a king: palace (noun) 8. envious: jealous (adjective)

3 Using New Vocabulary

- ❑ Note the group icon. To get students started, give your own example for the first word (such as *The poor miner and his kind wife lived in a hut.*). Tell students that this is your example and they should come up with their own sentence for *hut* as well.

- ❑ After students have finished, ask the different groups to give examples of some of their new sentences. Write some of the best examples on the board.

4 **Generating New Vocabulary Through Discussion**

Best Practice

Activating Prior Knowledge

This activity gives students the opportunity to link prior knowledge of vocabulary to new vocabulary they acquire through discussion with a partner about alternative story endings. This expanded vocabulary will be useful to them later, in their writing.

❏ Note the group icon. Divide students into mixed-ability groups of three or four. Encourage students to discuss as many alternative endings to the story as they can think of.

❏ After students have finished, ask volunteers to give examples of some of the new vocabulary they learned during this activity. Write the new words on the board.

Organizing Ideas

Best Practice

Scaffolding Instruction

The activities that follow systematically build on one another in order to prepare the student to write a one-paragraph ending for the story. These scaffolded activities help students learn to generate ideas for a story ending, learn about story elements, use a plot diagram, and write a good story title.

5 **Brainstorming Ideas for Your Story Ending**

❏ You might walk around the class during this activity, briefly discussing with each student some of his or her ideas.

❏ Remind students that they will be writing a one-paragraph story ending, and all the ideas that they eventually use should be related.

❏ After the students have finished, ask different students what they chose as their ending. Review possible answers to the questions in the Student Book.

ANSWER KEY

Answers may vary. Possible answers:

1. The brother decided to give the king his best horse. 2. He decided to give the king a gift because he wanted the king to reward him.
3. No, the king was not happy. He thought the brother was being greedy. 4. The king gave the miner's brother a bushel of corn for his horse.
5. The brother felt cheated.

Using Graphic Organizers

Best Practice

Organizational Tools

The next few activities will teach students how to use a five-part plot diagram to categorize the information in a story. Working with organizational tools such as this graphic organizer will help students visualize the construction of a good story. Students will then use that information to create their own plot diagram for a story ending they will write.

Strategy

Using a Plot Diagram

■ Review the information about using a plot diagram with the class.

■ Have students complete the following expansion activity.

EXPANSION ACTIVITY

■ Have students work in small groups to generate a plot diagram based on the unfinished story about the poor miner. Remind students that the five story elements can occur more than once in a story.

- After the students have finished, ask volunteers to give examples for each part. Ask students why their example is a good representation for that story element.

- Allow volunteers to put their plot diagrams on the board.

ANSWER KEY

Answers may vary. Possible answers:

Exposition: One day, a good and powerful king went for a ride alone in the forest.

Rising Action: After hours of riding, he got lost. He was tired, cold, and hungry.

Climax: Just before nightfall, he found the hut of a poor miner. "We are very poor," explained the miner's wife, "but we can give you potatoes for dinner and a blanket on the floor for a bed."

Falling Action: The king gratefully accepted the kind old woman's offer.

Resolution: He thanked the woman for her kindness and gave her a gold coin.

6 Creating a Plot Diagram

- ❏ Have students use their ideas from Activity 5 to create a plot diagram for their story ending.

- ❏ You might walk around the class during this activity, briefly discussing with each student the different parts of their plot diagrams.

- ❏ You might also want to have students, in pairs, discuss their diagrams with each other.

7 Limiting Information

- ❏ Allow students time to review their plot diagrams in light of the questions posed in this activity.

- ❏ Remind students that they are writing a one-paragraph story ending, so they need to carefully choose what they want to say.

- ❏ You might again walk around the class during this activity, briefly discussing each student's choices.

8 Sharing Your Ideas

Best Practice

Interacting with Others

Activities such as this one give students the opportunity to interact with a partner and receive constructive feedback on their story endings. Here, students work in pairs, using their plot diagrams to tell the story endings they have created. This interaction and the guided questions students answer help them clarify what works in their story endings and what does not. Students also get to see how their story ending is similar to and different from their peers' work.

- ❏ Note the pair icon. Give students time to tell their story ending to a partner.

- ❏ Have students use the questions in the Student Book to help them evaluate each other's work.

- ❏ Have volunteer pairs of students share some of the lessons they learned in this activity with the class.

Strategy

Writing a Title

- Review the information with the class.

- Have students give examples of great book and movie titles and write some examples on the board. These can serve as a model for students' story titles. Does the title hint at what is to come? Does the title give away too much?

9 Choosing the Best Title

- ❏ Tell students that there might be more than one correct choice.

❑ After students have had time to choose, ask for volunteers to explain their choices. Ask students to think of alternative titles as well, and write these on the board.

❑ Have students vote, by a show of hands, for their favorite title for the story.

ANSWER KEY

Answers may vary. Possible answers:

One possibility is *The Generous Brother and the Selfish Brother* because the story focuses on the character differences between the two brothers, especially at the end of the story. Another strong possibility is *The Miner and the King* as these two characters come from very different worlds, and their chance encounter is critical to the story.

Developing Cohesion and Clarity

WRITING ABOUT TWO EVENTS THAT OCCURRED IN THE PAST

- Review the information about using *when* and *while* with the class.

- Elicit additional examples of using *when* to introduce an action that interrupted another action in the past: I was sleeping *when* the phone rang.

- Elicit additional examples of using *while* to introduce the longer action: *While* I was sleeping, the phone rang.

- Elicit additional examples of using *while* to describe two actions that were in progress at the same time: *While* my friend was driving, I was looking at the map.

- Elicit additional examples of using *when* to describe an action that was followed by another action: *When* I received the package, I immediately called my friend.

1 Combining Sentences with *When* and *While*

Best Practice

Cultivating Critical Thinking

Activities such as these teach important critical thinking skills and provide varied opportunities for practicing them. In this activity, students are asked to combine two past tense sentences using *when* or *while*. In the following activities, students are asked to write sentences with *when* and *while*, combine sentences with *as soon as*, write sentences with *as soon as*, rewrite sentences using *then*, identify time words, and complete sentences with time words. The expansion activity after Activity 7 provides more opportunity for synthesizing and applying these skills.

- Review the activity directions and first example with the class.

- Remind students that more than one answer is possible and ask students for other possible

sentences for the first example (such as *The king was hunting when he got lost in the forest.* or *While the king was hunting, he got lost in the forest.*)

- After students have finished, review all possible answers with the class.

ANSWER KEY

Answers may vary. Possible answers:

1. When the king was hunting, he got lost in the forest. The king was hunting when he got lost in the forest. While the king was hunting, he got lost in the forest.
2. When the king saw the hut, he decided to ask for help.
3. While the miner was talking to the king, his wife was working at home. The miner was talking to the king while his wife was working at home. While his wife was working at home, the miner was talking to the king.
4. When the miner gave the potatoes to the king, the king was pleased.
5. When the king gave the coin to the woman, she was surprised.

2 Writing Sentences with *When* and *While*

- Review the activity directions and example sentence with the class.

- After students have finished, ask volunteers to share some of their sentences. Write examples on the board.

- Ask other students if they can think of any additional ways to write the same sentence.

USING *AS SOON AS*

- Review the information about using *as soon as* with the class.

- Have volunteers tell about something that happened to them in the past few days using *as soon as*.

3 Combining Sentences with *As Soon As*

❑ Review the activity directions and first example.

❑ After students have finished, review answers with the class.

ANSWER KEY

1. As soon as the brother heard the story, he decided to give the king a better gift.

2. As soon as the king talked to the brother, the king knew that he was a liar.

3. As soon as the king ate dinner, he fell asleep.

4. As soon as the miner got the farm, he quit his job.

---

4 Writing Sentences with *As Soon As*

❑ Review the activity directions with the class.

❑ After students have finished, ask volunteers to share some of their sentences. Write examples on the board.

USING *THEN*

■ Review the information about using *then* with the class.

■ Elicit additional examples of using *then* to clarify a time sequence. Ask students to recount three consecutive events in the past 24 hours.

---

5 Rewriting Sentences Using *Then*

❑ Review the activity directions and first example.

❑ After students have finished, review answers with the class.

ANSWER KEY

1. The king washed in the river. Then he thanked the woman and left.

2. The woman gave the king a plate of potatoes. Then she gave him a blanket.

3. The king gave the woman a coin. Then he gave the miner a house and a farm.

4. The brother found a bushel of potatoes. Then he took them to the king.

Strategy

Varying Time Words and Phrases

■ Review the information about varying time words with the class.

■ Encourage students to ask questions about anything they might not understand.

EXPANSION ACTIVITY

■ Have students work in small groups to write a short paragraph about events in their lives using all of the following time words and phrases: *when*, *while*, *then*, and *as soon as*. Write these words on the board. Each word or phrase must be used at least once.

■ After students have finished, have one student from each group read his or her paragraph aloud to the class. Allow other students to comment and ask questions.

■ Students' answers will obviously vary, but you can write a sample on the board.

SAMPLE PARAGRAPH

When I was a child, we had a fire in our house. *As soon as* I heard the fire alarm, I woke up. *While* I was running for the door, I fell down. Before the fire got to me, my father picked me up. After we got outside, I saw my mother and sister. *Then* the fire department arrived and put out the fire.

6 **Identifying Time Words**

- ❑ Note the pair icon. Tell students to list any time words that they learned in previous chapters as well as those from this chapter.

- ❑ Have students share their lists with a partner before discussing the activity as a class.

- ❑ After students have finished, ask volunteers to give a time word or phrase and then read the sentence or sentences from the story where it appears.

ANSWER KEY

After: After hours of riding in an unfamiliar part of the forest, he got lost.

Before: Just before nightfall, he found the hut of a poor miner.

When: She was cooking potatoes on the fire when she heard someone at the door. When he heard his brother's story, he was very upset.

Then: Then he stretched out on the floor and quickly fell asleep. Early the next morning, the king washed in the river and then returned to the hut. Then he left. Then she showed her husband the gold coin.

As soon as: As soon as the miner returned home, his wife told him about the visitor.

7 Completing Sentences with Time Words

- ❑ Review the activity directions and first example. Remind students that more than one answer is possible in some cases. Ask students for any alternative answers for the first example: *As soon as*.

- ❑ After students have finished, ask volunteers to share their answers with the class. Ask students if there are any alternative answers.

ANSWER KEY

Answers may vary. Possible answers:

1. When, As soon as 2. As soon as, When
3. when, as soon as 4. as soon as, when 5. As soon as, When 6. Then 7. while

REPRODUCIBLE EXPANSION ACTIVITY

- ■ Photocopy and distribute **Black Line Master 12**, "Time Words," on page BLM12 of this Teacher's Edition.

- ■ Tell students that they are going to complete a story using time words and phrases. At your discretion, have students work alone or in pairs.

- ■ After students have finished, have volunteers read their paragraphs. Discuss all possible answers for each example.

8 Writing the First Draft

- ❑ Review the activity directions with the class.

- ❑ Emphasize that a first draft is a rough form of writing. Students should try to write a complete, logical, one-paragraph ending to the story using time words to connect ideas and show a sequence of events, but they will revise this later. The content is the most important factor in the rough draft.

- ❑ Give students sufficient time to complete this assignment.

Revising for Content and Editing for Form

1 Revising for Content

❑ Remind students that this is a revision for content, length, and sequence. They will further edit the paragraph for punctuation, grammar, and form in Activity 2.

❑ After students have finished, review possible changes with the class.

❑ **Note to Instructor:** The following sample paragraph has been revised for both content and form and should be referred to for both Activities 1 and 2.

SAMPLE PARAGRAPH

While the miner's brother was riding home through the forest, he thought of a plan. He decided to give the king his best horse because he wanted the king to give him a gift like he gave his brother. So, as soon as he finished breakfast the next day, the brother went to the palace. The palace was not far from his house. When he got to the palace, he asked to see the king. The guard immediately took him to see the king. He gave the king his best horse. The king knew that this was not an honest gift. He smiled and gave the brother a sack of potatoes. What could the greedy brother do? He lifted the heavy bushel and sadly left the room. As he was leaving, he heard the king laughing.

USING EDITING SYMBOLS

■ Review the information about editing symbols with the class.

■ Make sure students understand that a sentence fragment is an incomplete sentence.

■ Elicit examples of each kind of mistake—a spelling error, a sentence fragment, an incorrect capitalization, something to be deleted, punctuation to be added. Write these on the board and have students tell you how to correct them.

2 Editing for Form

❑ Review the activity directions with the class.

❑ Remind students that they are editing for punctuation, grammar, and form now.

❑ After students have finished, review answers with the class.

❑ **Note to Instructor:** The Sample Paragraph following Activity 1 has been revised for both content and form and should be referred to for both Activities 1 and 2.

Evaluating Your Writing

3 Using a Rubric

Best Practice

Cultivating Critical Thinking

This activity requires students to critically evaluate their own writing based on both specific criteria and more general guidelines. In the following activity, students compare their story endings and make judgments and suggestions about the overall quality of the paragraphs.

❑ Review the rubric with your class. Using the completed sample paragraph from Activity 2, ask volunteers to evaluate it based on the first criteria: **Content**—*Paragraph concludes the folktale and contains all the relevant story elements.*

❑ Then have students use the rubric to evaluate the story endings they wrote.

4 Peer Sharing

Best Practice

Interacting with Others

Activities such as this one give students the opportunity to interact with a partner and receive constructive feedback on their writing. Here, students share their story endings with a partner, who compares it with his or her own writing and evaluates it in terms of the story elements studied in this chapter.

❑ Note the pair icon. Give students time to exchange story endings and read each other's work.

❑ Students should discuss how well the paragraphs work in terms of the story elements studied earlier. They should also compare their work for similarities and differences.

❑ Have volunteer pairs of students share their results with the class.

5 **Writing the Second Draft**

❑ Have students rewrite their story endings based on their own rubric evaluation from Activity 3, their peer conferences in Activity 4, and what they have learned in this chapter.

❑ Collect student paragraphs and make comments and corrections.

❑ Return students' paragraphs, then circulate through the classroom, discussing students' work and the written feedback you have given them.

What Do You Think?

Analyzing a Folktale Ending

■ Review the information about analyzing a folktale with the class.

■ As a class, answer the questions and discuss the moral or lesson of the story. Have students try to condense the lesson into a pithy statement, such as *What goes around comes around*; or *Generosity is rewarded, and greed is punished*.

EXPANSION ACTIVITY

■ Ask a volunteer to briefly tell the story of a folktale that he or she knows. Then as a class, discuss the following questions.

1. What is the moral of this story?

2. Does the story teach this lesson well?

■ Ask students to come up with a catchy moral or lesson for the folktale they just heard.

Focus on Testing — TOEFL® iBT

Borrowing Key Words from Short Readings

- Review the TOEFL®iBT information and hints for borrowing vocabulary with the class.

- Ask students why it is important to only borrow words and not copy entire phrases or sentences. Ask the students if they know the word *plagiarism* (the act of copying work from someone else and presenting it as your own).

Practice 1

After students have finished, ask volunteers to share some of the changes they made to their folktale ending based on the hints for borrowing vocabulary.

Practice 2

After students have finished, ask volunteers to share some of the sentences they wrote. Write some of the best examples on the board.

Writing with Computers

- Review the strategy for naming documents with the class.

- Do students agree with the advice about naming documents? Have they ever been unable to locate a document because they couldn't remember its name? Can they think of good advice for naming documents?

ANSWER KEY

Answers may vary. Possible answers to Practice 2:

1. The psychologist Carl Jung believed that folktales express the important beliefs in a culture and that all humans share a "collective unconscious."

2. Many folktales from different cultures share common themes and lessons, such as poor people being rewarded for their kindness and generosity.

3. Evil is another common element in folktales, but is usually defeated by a good person or animal.

1 Sharing Your Writing

❏ Have students read their story endings and then discuss the moral or lesson of their stories. Are there any differences in the messages of the stories or are they all basically the same?

❏ Have the students discuss the endings that they found most compelling or interesting. What did they like about the ending?

2 Writing the Beginning of a Story

❏ Note the pair icon. This activity can be done in class or as homework on two subsequent nights. The first night, all the students write a beginning, and the next night, they all write an ending to another student's beginning. Remind students to draw on everything they've learned in this chapter to complete the task.

❏ Students will write the beginning of a folktale that they know. The student who writes the ending doesn't necessarily have to know the folktale. This could allow for some interesting and surprising interpretations.

REPRODUCIBLE **EXPANSION ACTIVITY**

■ This expansion activity is a preparation for Activity 3, which follows.

■ Photocopy and distribute **Black Line Master 13**, "What's the Story?" on page BLM13 of this Teacher's Edition.

■ Tell students that they are going to read a folktale that has been altered.

■ After students have finished reading, ask them if they can identify the original story. What is different between the two versions? What is the same? Is the moral or lesson the same in the altered version?

■ If students are unfamiliar with the story, give a brief retelling.

■ Ask students to come up with a title for the story (such as *The Too Tall Girl*).

■ Ask students to come up with a catchy moral or lesson for the story (such as *Don't judge a book by its cover*; or *Beautiful things can come from unique packages*).

3 Rewriting a Folktale

❏ Note the group icon. Review the activity directions with the class.

❏ Advise students to change any well-known, central characters that would easily give the folktale away.

❏ If students seem to have difficulty with this activity, suggest that they rewrite one of the folktales discussed in this chapter.

4 Writing in Your Journal

❏ The topic in the Student Book can be used as a prompt for journal writing, but students can also generate their own ideas (such as *the most important lesson I ever learned*).

5 **Researching a Fable**

❑ Ideally this activity should be done using the Internet. If Internet access is not available to the students, have them use the library, or provide a book of Aesop's fables or another reference.

Self-Assessment Log

❑ Review the statements in the self-assessment log and then have students complete it.

7

Health

Chapter Opener

- ❑ Point out the title of this chapter, "Health." Ask students to discuss what being *healthy* means to them and to make predictions about what this chapter's theme is likely to be.

- ❑ Have students look at the photo. Explain that these people are exercising. Ask students how important exercising is to them and what their preferred exercise is (such as playing football or bicycling). Ask and answer the questions in Connecting to the Topic.

- ❑ Read the quotation or call on a student to read it. Share some of the content information about Thomas Jefferson with students. Then ask them if they agree or disagree with the statement. Ask students if they think anything is more important to them than health.

- ❑ Have students look at the description of the Writing Product. Tell them that as they work through the chapter, they should keep in mind that this will be the major writing assignment for this chapter.

Content Note

Born in Virginia, Thomas Jefferson was the son of a wealthy landowner, and his mother was a socialite. Jefferson was a true Renaissance man, who was skilled as an architect, linguist, and naturalist. He is best known, however, as a leader in the American Revolution against Great Britain, for drafting the Declaration of Independence at the age of 33, and later serving two terms as president of the United States. Jefferson retired to his mountaintop home, Monticello, with his wife Martha. Jefferson's tombstone reads, "author of the Declaration of American Independence, of the Statute of Virginia for religious freedom, and Father of the University of Virginia," as he requested.

❝ Health is worth more than learning. ❞

—Thomas Jefferson
Third president of the United States (1743–1826)

Chapter Overview

Writing Product

An informative paragraph about health treatments

Writing Process

- Build vocabulary for writing about health.
- Learn common suffixes.
- Use an idea map to generate and organize ideas.
- Write a topic sentence for an informative paragraph.
- Use restrictive relative clauses.
- Use transition words and phrases.
- Give reasons with *because* and infinitives of purpose.
- Use editing symbols.

Part 1: Before You Write

Exploring Ideas

Building Vocabulary

Organizing Ideas

Writing Topic Sentences

Part 2: Developing Writing Skills

Using Restrictive Relative Clauses

Using Transition Words and Phrases

Giving Reasons and Showing Purpose

Writing the First Draft

Part 3: Revising and Editing

Revising for Content

Editing for Form

Evaluating Your Writing

Peer Sharing

Writing the Second Draft

Focus on Testing

Part 4: Expansion Activities

Writing and Researching

What Do You Think?

Journal Writing

Self-Assessment Log

Exploring Ideas

> ### Best Practice
>
> **Making Use of Academic Content**
>
> Activities such as these contain authentic material that can lead to discussion of real-world issues. Students use definitions and information about traditional and modern medicine, practice doctor-patient conversations, and ask structured questions to generate discussion, create an idea map, choose a topic for their paragraphs, and write a topic sentence. This application of real-life content will help them prepare for the writing task ahead.

1 Discussing Modern and Traditional Medicine

- ❑ Note the group icon. Lead students in a brief discussion of the different types of medical treatments shown in the photographs, such as the use of acupuncture, advanced technology, traditional herbs, and modern pharmaceuticals. You might want to write some of these words on the board.

- ❑ Have students work in small groups to answer the questions.

- ❑ After students have finished, continue the discussion by asking for volunteers to share their answers and opinions with the class. Encourage students to debate the merits of the various treatments.

Defining Terms

- ❑ Review the definitions of *traditional medicine* and *modern medicine* with the class.

- ❑ Check comprehension by modeling and eliciting examples of both types of medicine, such as Chinese herbs and acupuncture for traditional medicine, and x-rays and drugs for modern medicine.

2 Discussing the Topic

- ❑ Note the group icon. Have students work in small groups to discuss the questions.

- ❑ After students have finished, broaden the discussion to include the entire class. Have students share experiences they have had with different kinds of remedies. You might want to provide personal examples or knowledge to help begin the discussion.

Building Vocabulary

3 Using a Vocabulary Chart

- ❑ Review the activity directions with the class. To get the students started, discuss where the word *symptoms* would go: *Nouns*.

- ❑ After students have finished, ask volunteers to read the conversations aloud. Then review where the underlined words would go in the chart.

- ❑ Check comprehension by asking students to create sentences using the new vocabulary, such as *My symptoms are a sore throat and aches; The last time I had the flu, I had a high fever; What do you do for a sore throat?*

- ❑ Tell students they should continue to add vocabulary to their charts as they encounter new words related to the topic.

ANSWER KEY

Nouns: fever, treatment, reliever, healer, teas, pain, acupuncture, herb, needles

Verbs: hurt, relieve, take, treat

Adjectives: sore, painful, safe, herbal, effective

Adverb: effectively

Cultivating Critical Thinking

Activities such as these teach a particular critical thinking skill and provide opportunities for practicing it. In this case, the skill of changing the part of speech of a word by adding a suffix is presented, and then students are asked to fill in a chart with pairs of related words changed by a suffix. They are also asked to identify the part of speech before and after the suffix change. The expansion activity after Activity 4 provides more opportunity for synthesizing and applying this skill.

ADDING SUFFIXES

- Review the suffix information and examples with the class. Remind students that suffixes are always added to the end of a word.

- Elicit additional examples of verb + suffix -*er* = noun: *singer*.

- Elicit additional examples of noun + suffix -*ly* = adjective or adverb: *cowardly*.

- Elicit examples of any words with the suffixes -*ful*, -*ment*, and -*al*: *faithful, retirement, communal*.

4 Identifying Word Pairs

- ❑ Review the activity directions and first example with the class. Ask students to identify what part of speech each word was before and after the suffix change.

- ❑ After students have finished, ask volunteers to share their answers with the class, identifying the parts of speech.

ANSWER KEY

Answers may vary. Possible answers:

relieve/reliever – verb/noun; heal/healer – verb/noun; pain/painful – noun/adjective; herb/herbal – noun/adjective; hurt/hurtful – verb/adjective;

safe/safely – adjective/adverb; effective/effectively – adjective/adverb

EXPANSION ACTIVITY

- ■ Photocopy and distribute **Black Line Master 14** "Word Pairs" on page BLM14 of this Teacher's Edition.

- ■ Tell students that they are going to look at a list of words they have encountered in previous chapters. They will identify the word's part of speech, change the word by adding a suffix, and identify the new part of speech. They can also add their own examples to the list.

- ■ After students have finished, have volunteers share their answers. Make a list of any student-generated examples on the board.

Organizing Ideas

Organizing Information

Activities such as these will teach students how to use an idea map to help them organize their ideas for an informational paragraph. Working with organizational tools such as these helps students visualize the connections between ideas in a paragraph. Students will then use that information to choose a topic and write a topic sentence. Idea maps are an excellent tool for students to use in organizing information in their own writing.

Strategy

Using Idea Maps

- ■ Review the information and example with the class.

- ■ Ask students if this kind of organizational tool is something that helps them develop their thoughts. Why or why not?

5 **Creating a Graphic Organizer**

- ❑ Review the sample idea map with students. Ask students for other traditional medicines they know about and record their ideas on a map. Show how the names of treatments are put on the second tier of the map, and how the details about each particular treatment are written on the other tiers.

- ❑ You might walk around the class during this activity, briefly discussing with each student some of his or her ideas.

- ❑ After the students have finished, ask volunteers to draw their idea maps on the board. Are the connections clear to everyone?

6 **Choosing a Topic**

- ❑ The suggestions in the Student Book are intended to help students come up with ideas for their paragraphs. They may also generate other ideas of their own.

7 **Brainstorming and Evaluating Ideas**

- ❑ Remind students that they are going to write an informational paragraph and all the ideas that are connected in their idea maps should be related to each other.

- ❑ You could choose to have students pair up and discuss their ideas after they have written them down.

- ❑ You might walk around the class during this activity, briefly discussing with each student some of his or her ideas.

Writing Topic Sentences

Strategy

Writing a Good Topic Sentence

- ■ Review the information about writing a good topic sentence with the class.

- ■ Remind students that a topic sentence should also create reader interest in the rest of the paragraph. The topic sentence should draw the reader in.

8 **Choosing the Best Topic Sentence**

- ❑ Review the activity directions with the class.

- ❑ After the students have finished, ask for volunteers to answer and explain why they chose that sentence.

ANSWER KEY

Paragraph 1: The best answer is sentence #2. It is general enough to cover a variety of remedies for different ailments, but is still very much on subject.

Paragraph 2: The best answer is sentence #1. The sentence meets all the criteria for a topic sentence and is, importantly, interesting and draws the reader in.

Paragraph 3: The best answer is sentence #3. The other sentences are too narrow in focus to be effective topic sentences.

9 **Writing a Draft Topic Sentence**

- ❑ After the students have finished using their idea maps to write a topic sentence, you might have them work in pairs and compare their results.

- ❑ You might walk around the class during this activity, briefly discussing with each pair of students their choices. Do their topic sentences capture the main idea of the various ideas they have gathered for their paragraphs? Are their partners interested in reading more after reading the topic sentence?

Developing Cohesion and Clarity

Best Practice

Scaffolding Instruction

The scaffolded activities that follow prepare the students for success in their writing. The various activities—using restrictive relative clauses, using transitional words and phrases, and giving reasons and showing purpose—systematically build on one another in order to prepare the student to write an informational paragraph on traditional medicine. The expansion activity after Activity 5 is a final preparatory step before students write a first draft.

USING RESTRICTIVE RELATIVE CLAUSES

- Review with the class the information about and examples of combining short sentences with *who* and *that*.

- Model and elicit additional examples of sentences using the relative pronoun *who* to make longer, more natural sentences about people. For example, you could model: *I know a lot of people who practice traditional medicine.*

- Elicit additional examples of sentences using the relative pronoun *that* to make longer, more natural sentences about people and things. Model: *There is no one treatment that is a certain cure for cancer.*

1 Combining Sentences with Relative Pronouns

- ❏ Review the activity directions and first example with the class.

- ❏ After students have finished, review all possible answers with the class.

ANSWER KEY

Answers may vary. Possible answers:

1. Acupuncture is an ancient treatment <u>that</u> was developed in China. 2. She is a very skilled acupuncturist <u>who/that</u> has cured many people. 3. People <u>who/that</u> suffer from different diseases look for good acupuncturists. 4. Acupuncturists also use herbs <u>that</u> help treat health problems. 5. Poor digestion is a common health problem <u>that</u> can be treated with acupuncture.

2 Completing Sentences with Relative Clauses

- ❏ Review the activity directions and first example with the class.

- ❏ After students have finished, ask volunteers to share some of their sentences. Write examples on the board.

ANSWER KEY

Answers may vary. Possible answers:

1. There are many traditional remedies that can cure common health problems. 2. People who are trained in Chinese medicine often use herbs to treat diseases. 3. I knew a woman who cured herself of cancer by drinking tea. 4. There are many plants that have beneficial effects. 5. My friend goes to a doctor who combines modern and traditional medicine. 6. My grandmother uses an herb that settles an upset stomach. 7. I know someone who gets a massage every week. 8. There are some new medicines that are very promising in the treatment of cancer. 9. I once used a traditional treatment that did nothing for me. 10. I once read a story about a man who traveled all the way from Argentina to China for his treatment.

USING TRANSITION WORDS AND PHRASES: *IN ADDITION, FOR EXAMPLE* AND *HOWEVER*

- Review the information about transition words and phrases with the class.

- Elicit additional examples of sentences using *in addition* to add information. Model: *Yoga helps me to stay in shape. In addition, it helps my asthma.*

- Elicit additional examples of sentences using *for example* to give specific examples: *Acupuncture can be very effective in pain management. For example, it is good for treating dental pain and pain from arthritis.*

- Elicit additional examples of sentences using *however* to give contrasting information: *It is important that the best health care be available. However, it must also be affordable.*

3 Completing Sentences with Transition Words

- ❑ Review the activity directions and first example.

- ❑ After students have finished, review answers with the class.

ANSWER KEY

1. There are many Chinese acupuncturists in Canada. Many of them studied acupuncture in China and then immigrated to Canada. In addition, many Canadian doctors are now giving acupuncture treatments. 2. I often drink herbal teas when I am sick. However, if I am very sick or have a fever, I take modern medicine. 3. Some people in California use many traditional treatments from various parts of the world. For example, they use remedies and treatments from China and India. 4. My grandmother often goes to an old lady who gives her very expensive treatments. However, these treatments don't usually help her. 5. I use lemon juice for colds. I put it in a cup of warm water and drink it several times a day. In addition, I take it for sore throats and fevers.

4 Writing Sentences with Transition Words

- ❑ Review the activity directions with the class.

- ❑ You might like to have students work in pairs for this activity. Have one read the sentence and the other add another sentence that begins with *For example, In addition,* or *However.* Then have them switch roles.

- ❑ After students have finished, ask volunteers to share some of their sentences. Write examples on the board.

ANSWER KEY

Answers may vary. Possible answers:

1. I don't use traditional treatments. However, my sister thinks they are very effective. 2. Many herbal teas are good for digestion. In addition, they can be very calming. 3. She went to a nutritionist. However, he didn't have the answers she was looking for. 4. Massage therapists can help you overcome headaches. However, the treatment can be quite expensive. 5. It's important to eat healthful foods. For example, fresh fruits, organic vegetables, and whole grains are all good for you.

GIVING REASONS AND SHOWING PURPOSE

- Review the information on using *because* to give reasons and infinitives to show reason or purpose.

- Model and elicit additional examples of *because* to give reasons: *I changed my doctor because he was totally against traditional medicine.*

- Model and elicit additional examples of *because* at the beginning of a sentence to give reasons: *Because my back hurts, I see a chiropractor once a month.*

- Model and elicit additional examples of an infinitive (to + verb) to show reason or purpose: *She drinks chamomile tea to help her sleep.*

5 Identifying Clauses That Show Reason and Purpose

❑ Review the activity directions.

❑ You may want to model pronunciation and intonation by reading the paragraph aloud. Then invite volunteers to take turns reading parts of the paragraph aloud for the class.

❑ After students have finished, review answers with the class.

ANSWER KEY

1. <u>because</u> it kills germs 2. Because scientists haven't found an easily available medicine that kills viruses that cause colds, 3. to treat, to cure, to help

EXPANSION ACTIVITY

■ Divide the class into two groups. Assign one group the role of supporting traditional medicine and the other that of opposing traditional medicine. Tell students to leave aside personal opinions for this activity.

■ Have each group write as many sentences as they can using restrictive relative clauses, transitional words and phrases, and *because* and infinitives to show reason or purpose. Each groups' sentences should support the position on traditional medicine that you have assigned them.

■ You might begin this activity by writing an example of both the pro and con positions on the board, such as: *Traditional medicine is very beneficial <u>because</u> it helps people <u>who</u> cannot afford to go to doctors. Many people talk about the benefits of traditional medicine; <u>however</u>, there is little scientific evidence to <u>demonstrate</u> this.*

■ After students have finished, have volunteers from each group read a sentence aloud to the class. Does the sentence successfully support that group's position? Allow other students to comment and ask questions.

■ Write some of the best example sentences on the board.

6 Writing the First Draft

❑ Review the activity directions with the class. Remind students that they learned how to use *also* to add information in Chapter 1.

❑ Students should write a first draft of an informational paragraph about traditional medicine, but remind them that they will revise this later. The content is the most important factor in the rough draft.

Revising for Content and Editing for Form

1 Revising for Content

❑ Remind students that this is a revision for content and for use of transition words. They will further edit the paragraph for form using editing symbols in Activity 2.

❑ You might have students work in pairs for this activity, then compare their answers with another pair.

❑ After students have finished, review possible changes with the class.

❑ **Note to Instructor:** The following Sample Paragraph has been revised for both content and form and should be referred to for both Activities 1 and 2.

SAMPLE PARAGRAPH

Scientists don't have a modern drug to cure cancer. However, some people can cure themselves of cancer with traditional treatments. For example, I know a woman who cured herself of cancer by fasting. She didn't eat for one month, and then she slowly began to eat again. When she completed the fast, she had completely cured herself of cancer. In addition, I read about a man who cured his cancer using a traditional Chinese diet. As soon as he started the diet, he began to get better. Even though there is no modern cure for cancer, some traditional cures may exist.

USING EDITING SYMBOLS

■ Review the information on editing symbols with the class.

■ Make sure students are clear on all meanings (such as run-on sentence = two or more sentences inappropriately written as one).

■ Review the editing symbols students learned in Chapter 6: *sp* = wrong spelling, *sf* = sentence fragment, / = use lowercase, ℐ = delete, and ⊙/∧ = add punctuation.

2 Editing for Form

❑ Review the activity directions with the class.

❑ Remind students that they are editing for punctuation, grammar, and form now. Students should use any editing symbols they've learned up to this point.

❑ After students have finished, review answers with the class.

❑ **Note to Instructor:** The Sample Paragraph following Activity 1 has been revised for both content and form and should be referred to for both Activities 1 and 2.

3 Editing Practice

❑ Review the activity directions and first example with the class. Explain that item 1 includes a new editing symbol.

❑ Remind students that they will be editing based on the editing symbols they've learned in this chapter.

❑ You might like to have students work in pairs to complete this activity.

❑ After students have finished, review edits with the class.

ANSWER KEY

1. Many people in the Philippines drink herbal teas. 2. The healer gave a foot massage to my friend. 3. Three days ago he had a stomachache. 4. His leg did not heal. 5. My friend didn't like to go to doctors, so he went to a psychic.

Evaluating Your Writing

4 Using a Rubric

Best Practice

Cultivating Critical Thinking

This activity requires students to critically evaluate their informative paragraphs based on both specific criteria and more general guidelines. In the following activity, students conference with a partner to compare their paragraphs and make judgments and suggestions about the overall quality of the writing.

❑ Review the rubric with your class. Using the completed sample paragraph from Activity 2, ask volunteers to evaluate it based on the first criteria: **Content** – *Paragraph presents enough information about the topic so that the reader has a very clear understanding of it*.

❑ Then have students use the rubric to evaluate the informational paragraph they wrote.

5 Peer Sharing

Best Practice

Interacting with Others

Activities such as this give students the opportunity to interact with a partner and receive constructive feedback on their writing. Here, students share their informative paragraphs with a partner who compares it with his or her own writing and evaluates it for clarity.

❑ Note the pair icon. Give students time to exchange paragraphs and read each other's work.

❑ Students should discuss how well the paragraphs work according to the criteria in the rubric.

❑ Have students share the ideas they found interesting in each other's work with the class.

Writing with Computers

■ Review the information with the class.

■ Do students agree with the advice about saving writing? Do any of the students have their computers automatically set to save information? If so, how often? Do any of the students have any stories to tell about losing work they've done? What happened? Do any students use other strategies to safeguard their work, such as always printing out a copy?

6 Writing the Second Draft

❑ Have students rewrite their paragraphs based on their own rubric evaluations from Activity 4, their peer conferences in Activity 5, and what they've learned in this chapter.

❑ Collect student paragraphs and make comments and corrections.

❑ Return students' paragraphs, then circulate through the classroom, discussing students' work and your feedback.

Focus on Testing   TOEFL® iBT

Transition Words and Phrases

- Review the TOEFL® iBT information and sample prompts with the class.

- Ask students why this part of the test is called the "independent" task. Elicit that the prompts are merely starting points for the task and the student is on his or her own for 30 minutes.

- Ask students if they noticed the clear call for transition words in Prompt 1 and time or narration transitions in Prompt 2 before they were pointed out. Elicit from the students that it is very important to read all TOEFL® iBT directions very carefully because they contain valuable information about completing the task.

Practice

- Review the activity directions with the class.

- After students have finished, collect student paragraphs and make comments and corrections.

Best Practice

Activating Prior Knowledge

These activities give students the opportunity to link prior knowledge to new information they acquire through discussion with a partner and research. Working in pairs, they can learn from their partners' prior knowledge and together they can organize and present their new concepts to the class. In the following activity, students present to the class new information they acquired through research. The class in turn is given the opportunity to link their prior knowledge to the new information that their classmates provide.

1 Sharing Your Writing

❑ Note the group icon. Have students use photographs, drawings, or other materials to complement their paragraphs. They might also want to organize the book by different themes, such as physical therapies and traditional medicines.

❑ Have students determine a title for their book and a cover photograph or illustration, as well. Encourage students to be as creative as possible. Allow them to determine if they prefer the paragraphs to be typed or handwritten.

❑ You might provide manuals on herbal remedies, acupuncture, and other kinds of traditional remedies as source material for the students to use during this activity.

2 Writing About Health Treatments

❑ Be aware that some students may have had very serious illnesses or deaths in their families and may not wish to participate in this activity. Allow students the option of writing on another related subject of their choice.

3 Writing in Your Journal

❑ The topics in the Student Book can be used as prompts for journal writing, but students can also generate their own ideas related to the theme and content of the chapter, such as *my first experience with traditional medicine*.

What Do You Think?

Analyzing the Differences Between Modern and Traditional Medicine

- Review the activity directions and chart with the class.

- Write an identical chart on the board. After students have finished working in pairs, ask them to share the differences they came up with. Put student responses in the appropriate columns on the board and discuss them as a class.

- What are some of the additional features that students came up with? Ask students what they think are the strongest pros and cons for both modern and traditional medicine.

- Have students make sentences with the information on the board using restrictive relative clauses, transitional words and phrases, and *because* and infinitives to show reason or purpose. For example: *There are many traditional remedies <u>that</u> are inexpensive; Most practitioners of traditional medicine are honest and try to help people. <u>However</u>, there are some who take advantage of people and steal their money.*

ANSWER KEY

Answers may vary. Possible answers:

Traditional Medicine	Modern Medicine
inexpensive	expensive
doesn't always require specialized training	requires years of formal training
can be dangerous	surgery can sometimes be dangerous
can be used to treat all kinds of illnesses, including "spiritual" diseases	is more impersonal and artificial
is personal and natural	is controlled by the government
is not controlled by the government	doctors are sometimes guilty of malpractice
practitioners sometimes cheat people	

EXPANSION ACTIVITY

- This activity can be done individually or with a partner.

- Photocopy and distribute **Black Line Master 15**, "KWL Chart," on page BLM15 of this Teacher's Edition. Print and distribute KWL Chart.

- Tell students that they are going to chose something about either traditional or modern medicine that they would like to learn more about, such as CAT scans or acupuncture. They will use a graphic organizer to note what it is they want to learn. Then they'll do research online or in the library, and complete the chart with information about what they learned.

- After students have finished, have them share their charts with the class. Encourage the class to comment and ask questions.

4 **Researching Traditional Health Treatments**

- ❑ Ideally this activity should be done using the Internet. If Internet access is not available to the students, have them use the library.

- ❑ This activity offers another opportunity for the students to put together a booklet similar to the one in Activity 1.

Self-Assessment Log

- ❑ Review the statements in the self-assessment log and then have students complete it.

8

Entertainment and the Media

Chapter Opener

❑ Point out the title of this chapter, "Entertainment and the Media." Ask students to discuss what *media* means (mass communication, such as newspapers, magazines, radio, or television) and to make predictions about what this chapter's theme is likely to be.

❑ Have students look at the photo. Explain that these people are enjoying different types of entertainment and media. Ask students how important entertainment and media are to them. Ask and answer the questions in Connecting to the Topic.

❑ Read the quotation or call on a student to read it. Share some of the content information about Lady Mary Wortley Montagu with students. Then ask them if they agree or disagree with the statement. Ask students if they enjoy reading and how important it is to them. How does it compare to other kinds of entertainment and media?

❑ Have students look at the description of the Writing Product. Tell them that as they work through the chapter, they should keep in mind that this will be the major writing assignment for this chapter.

Content Note

Born Mary Pierrepont, Lady Mary Wortley Montagu was a poet and prolific letter writer. She is well known for her correspondence with Mary Astell, an early champion of women's rights. She married Wortley Montagu, who later served as British ambassador to the Ottoman Empire.

❝ No entertainment is so cheap as reading, nor any pleasure so lasting. ❞

—Lady Mary Wortley Montagu
English letter writer (1689–1762)

Chapter Overview

Writing Product

A one-paragraph movie review

Writing Process

- Categorize movies by genre.
- Use a story web.
- Identify story elements.
- Write a title for a movie review.
- Use adjectives to describe character and setting.
- Use appositives.
- Use the historical present tense.

Part 1: Before You Write

Exploring Ideas

Building Vocabulary

Organizing Ideas

Part 2: Developing Writing Skills

Using Adjectives

Using Appositives

Using the Historical Present Tense

Writing the First Draft

Part 3: Revising and Editing

Revising for Content

Editing for Form

Evaluating Your Writing

Peer Sharing

Writing the Second Draft

Focus on Testing

What Do You Think?

Part 4: Expansion Activities

Writing and Researching

Journal Writing

Self-Assessment Log

Exploring Ideas

Best Practice

Activating Prior Knowledge

These activities give students the opportunity to link prior knowledge to new information they acquire through categorizing movies by genre and discussing movies in groups. Working in groups, they can learn from their partners' movie knowledge and together they can organize and present their preferences to the class. The class, in turn, is given the opportunity to link their prior knowledge to the new information that their classmates provide. Extensive use of adjectives will also help prepare students for the writing task ahead.

1 Categorizing Movies

❑ Review the activity directions and first example with the class.

❑ Before students do the activity, review the meanings of the different genres. Elicit examples of each type, such as *action = Mission Impossible*; *comedy = Dumb and Dumber*; *drama = Basic Instinct*; *fantasy = The Chronicles of Narnia*; *horror = The Exorcist*; *musical = Chicago*; and *science fiction = Star Wars*.

❑ After students have finished, review answers with the class. Ask how many students have seen each film. What did they think of it?

ANSWER KEY

1. science fiction 2. comedy 3. fantasy
4. musical 5. drama 6. horror 7. action

2 Discussing Movies

❑ Note the group icon. Have students work in small groups to discuss the questions.

❑ After students have finished, broaden the discussion to include the entire class. Have students share movie experiences they have had. You might want to provide personal examples to help begin the discussion.

Building Vocabulary

3 Identifying Adjectives

❑ You may want to have students work in mixed-level (strong/weak) pairs to complete this activity.

❑ Ask students to share which words they had to look up in a dictionary. Either model using each word in a sentence to clarify its meaning or ask volunteers to do so.

❑ Ask volunteers to share their favorite movie with the class and the adjectives they chose to describe it. Allow students to comment and ask questions.

4 Identifying Positive and Negative Adjectives

❑ Review the activity directions with the class. You might want to do the first example with the class: *ambitious* = positive.

❑ If groups are unable to determine the meaning of an adjective, explain as necessary.

❑ After students have finished, ask volunteers to share their answers with the class.

ANSWER KEY

Positive Characteristics: ambitious, brave, brilliant, courageous, fun-loving, funny, gorgeous, handsome, hardworking, independent, kind, loyal, peaceful, sexy, talented, well-built

Negative Characteristics: angry, egotistical, evil, stubborn, wicked

Open to interpretation: brawny, childlike, crazy, innocent, ordinary, shy, stocky, talkative

EXPANSION ACTIVITY

- Tell students that they are going to use a graphic organizer to arrange adjectives about a topic and then use them in sentences.

- Photocopy and distribute **Black Line Master 16**, "Adjectives," on page BLM16 of this Teacher's Edition.

- Divide students into small groups (two to three people). Have them look at the list of famous movies and actors on the handout and choose three of them. Tell them that they will then complete a word web for each, writing the name of the movie or actor in the larger oval and adjectives in the smaller circles.

- Tell students they can refer to the adjectives used in Activities 3 and 4, as well as any other adjectives they can think of. Then, in the box below the ovals, they should write at least two sentences about each movie or actor using the adjectives.

- Tell students to be prepared to share their answers with the class.

- After students have finished, ask volunteers to share their answers. Write some of the best examples on the board.

5 Choosing Adjectives

❑ Answers will vary. Have volunteers share their answers with the class and ask them to support their answers with examples and reasons.

6 Writing Adjectives

❑ Answers will vary. Have students use a thesaurus to help them think of related terms and synonyms.

❑ Have volunteers share their answers with the class and make a list of new adjectives on the board.

❑ Model or ask volunteers to create sentences using each new word to clarify its meaning.

Organizing Ideas

Best Practice

Organizing Information

Activities such as these will teach students how to use a story web to help them organize their ideas for a one-paragraph movie review. Working with such organizational tools will help students visualize the different story elements and organize their notes around each element. Story webs are great tools for students to use in organizing information for their own writing.

USING A STORY WEB

- Review the model story web with the class. Explain to students that this kind of organizational tool is something that will help them organize their thoughts.

- Make sure that all terms are clear to the students. To check comprehension, ask volunteers to explain what each story element means in his or her own words.

- You might want to choose a very well-known movie and do a brief story web on the board as a class.

7 Creating a Story Web

❑ Remind students that they are going to write a one-paragraph movie review of their favorite movie, and explain that this activity will help them organize their ideas for the paragraph.

❑ You could choose to have students pair up and discuss their story webs after they have created them.

❑ You might walk around the class during this activity, briefly discussing with each student some of his or her ideas.

8 Identifying Story Elements in a Movie Review

❑ Review the activity directions and first answer with the class.

- ❑ Discuss whether students have seen and what they know about the two movies they will read about in this activity: *The Lord of the Rings* and *E.T.*

- ❑ After students have finished, have them get into small groups to complete Activity 9.

- ❑ Note that answers for Activity 8 will not be given until Activity 9 is completed.

9 Discussing Movie Reviews

- ❑ Note the group icon. Have students share their answers from Activity 8 with the other members of their group. Any differences should be discussed to determine what the best answer is.

- ❑ After students have finished, have volunteers share their answers with the class.

ANSWER KEY

1. *The Lord of the Rings* 2. an imaginary place called Middle Earth 3. You'll have to see the movie to find out what happens. Does this brave group destroy the ring and save the world from darkness? Or do the evil lords win? 4. fantasy 5. Gandalf tells Frodo that he must take the ring to Mordor, an evil, far away place, and destroy it. Along the way, they meet many dangerous creatures. 6. The movie is quite frightening in places because the special effects are realistic. 7. Hobbits, Gandalf the wizard, Lord Sauron, Frodo.

1. *E.T.: The Extra-Terrestrial* 2. in the 1980s, in a small American town 3. They go to the woods to meet the spaceship that will take E.T. home, and in a beautiful scene, they say good-bye. 4. science fiction 5. Because a group of scientists are searching for E.T. in order to study him, Elliot and E.T. have to escape from the scientists by bicycle. 6. I found everything I like best about a movie in *E.T.*: wonderful characters, suspense, magic, and an ending that moved me to tears. 7. Elliot, E.T., scientists

10 Choosing the Best Title

- ❑ Review the activity directions with the class.

- ❑ After the students have finished, ask for volunteers to answer and explain why they chose that title. What is it exactly about the title that attracts them? What is their least favorite title? Why?

- ❑ Poll the class to find the overall favorite title. What is the least favorite title?

WRITING MOVIE TITLES

- ■ Review the information about writing movie titles and examples with the class. Make sure students understand the meaning of *italicized*.

- ■ Ask volunteers to write the name of their favorite movie on the board. Allow other students to comment before you make any corrections.

11 Punctuating Movie Titles

- ❑ Review the activity directions and first example with the class. Make sure students understand that the parentheses should be removed.

- ❑ After the students have finished, ask for volunteers to write the sentences containing the movie titles on the board. Allow other students to comment before you make any corrections.

ANSWER KEY

1. You should see *The Seven Dwarfs*, a classic Disney film.
2. The Chinese actor Chow Yun-Fat was in *Anna and the King*.
3. The Italian movie *Life is Beautiful* won several awards.
4. Sandra Bullock starred in *While You Were Sleeping*.
5. One of the most famous horror movies of all time is *The Exorcist*.

12 Writing a Title

❑ After the students have finished, ask for volunteers to write their movie review titles on the board. Allow other students to comment before you make any corrections.

Developing Cohesion and Clarity

Strategy

Using Adjectives

- Review the strategy with the class.

- Ask students if they have ever been influenced by a movie review to see or not see a film. What was it about the review that made it so powerful? Can they recall any compelling adjectives that were used in a review they read?

1 Completing Sentences with Adjectives

- ❏ Review the activity directions and first example with the class. Tell students that they can use adjectives from previous activities or adjectives of their own choosing.

- ❏ After students have finished, ask volunteers to share some of their sentences. Write examples on the board.

ANSWER KEY

Answers may vary. Possible answers:

1. *Star Wars* is an exciting science-fiction movie.
2. *Dracula* is a frightening horror movie about an evil vampire.
3. *Titanic* is a touching love story about a couple on a sinking ship.
4. *The Lord of the Rings* is a magical fantasy about an incredible journey.

2 Using Adjectives in a Sentence

- ❏ Have students use the sentences they've just completed in Activity 1 as models for writing their own sentences.

- ❏ You could choose to have students pair up and discuss their sentences after they have finished.

- ❏ After students have finished, ask volunteers to share some of their sentences with the class.

- ❏ Ask volunteers to contribute other adjectives that describe the movies mentioned.

3 Writing Phrases with Adjectives

- ❏ Note the group icon. Review the activity directions and examples with the class.

- ❏ Tell students that they don't need to write complete sentences here. The purpose of this activity is to write descriptive phrases using as many different adjectives as they can.

- ❏ After students have finished, review possible answers with the class and write some of the best phrases on the board.

ANSWER KEY

Answers may vary. Possible answers:

Luke Skywalker – a brave and adventurous space pilot

Hannibal Lecter – a gruesome serial killer

Evita – a beautiful, charismatic leader

USING APPOSITIVES

- Review the information about using appositives with the class.

- Elicit additional examples of appositives using the phrases students generated in Activity 3, such as *Luke Skywalker, a brave and adventurous space pilot, is one of the central characters in* Star Wars.

Best Practice

Cultivating Critical Thinking

Activities such as these teach important critical thinking skills and provide varied opportunities for practicing them. In this case, students are asked to identify appositives in two different movie reviews. In the following activities, students are asked to combine and then write their own sentences using appositives.

4 **Identifying Appositives**

❑ Review the activity directions with the class. Identify the first appositive with the class: *my favorite book*.

❑ After students have finished, have volunteers read sentences from the reviews aloud and then identify the appositive, or lack of an appositive, in each sentence. Allow other students to comment before you make any corrections.

ANSWER KEY

The Lord of the Rings, <u>my favorite book,</u> recently became my favorite movie. This fantasy takes place in an imaginary place called Middle Earth. Many strange creatures live there. Some of them are good, and some are wicked. One group are innocent, peaceful creatures called Hobbits. A small Hobbit named Frodo inherits a very old ring when his uncle disappears. Gandalf, <u>a kind wizard,</u> says that the ring belongs to the evil Lord Sauron. Gandalf tells Frodo that he must take the ring to Mordor, <u>an evil, far away place,</u> and destroy it. The story is about Frodo's trip with three other Hobbits and a number of other creatures. They travel through mountains, snow, darkness, forests, and rivers. Along the way, they meet many dangerous creatures. The movie is quite frightening in places because the special effects are very realistic. You'll have to see the movie to find out what happens. Does this brave group destroy the ring and save the world from darkness? Or do the evil lords win?

One of my favorite movies is *E.T.: The Extra-Terrestrial*, <u>a touching science fiction story about the friendship of a young boy and E.T., a creature from outer space</u>. It takes place in the 1980s, in a small American town. When E.T.'s spaceship leaves Earth without him, he meets Elliot, <u>a boy who becomes his friend</u>. Since E.T. is very homesick, Elliot decides to help him contact his friends. Because a group of scientists are searching for E.T. in order to study him, Elliot and E.T. have to escape from the scientists by bicycle. They go to the woods to meet the spaceship that will take E.T. home, and in a beautiful scene, they say good-bye. I found everything I like best about a movie in *E.T.*: wonderful characters, suspense, magic, and an ending that moved me to tears.

5 **Using Appositives to Combine Sentences**

❑ Review the activity directions and first example with the class. Remind students to pay special attention to their use of commas.

❑ After students have finished, review answers with the class. You may want to model pronunciation and intonation by reading the sentences aloud. Then invite volunteers to take turns reading the sentences aloud for the class.

ANSWER KEY

1. *Gone with the Wind*, a film about the U.S. Civil War, takes place in the south of the United States.
2. In *Jurassic Park*, a hair-raising thriller, the dinosaurs seem real.
3. Cal Hockley, a rich but evil man, is Rose's fiancé in *Titanic*.
4. *Cold Mountain*, a story about two lovers separated by war, is a tragedy.
5. In *Shakespeare in Love*, Gwyneth Paltrow, a famous American actress, plays a woman who pretends to be a man.

6 **Writing Sentences with Appositives**

❑ Review the activity directions with the class. Model an example for the students by writing a sentence on the board about a popular movie they might know. Read the sentence aloud and identify the appositive.

❑ After students have finished, ask volunteers to share some of their sentences. Write examples on the board.

USING THE HISTORICAL PRESENT TENSE

■ Review the information about using the historical present tense with the class.

■ Model and elicit additional examples of historical present tense: *In The Da Vinci Code, a murder in the Louvre museum reveals a plot to expose an ancient secret.*

7 **Completing Sentences with the Correct Verb Tense**

❑ Remind students that when discussing actions and thoughts that occur in books and films, we use the present tense.

❑ Review the activity directions and first example with the class.

❑ After students have finished, ask volunteers to read the sentences aloud with the correct verb tense. Allow other students to comment before you make any corrections.

ANSWER KEY

1. is 2. plays 3. lives 4. becomes 5. tries
6. shows 7. is 8. decides

Best Practice

Scaffolding Instruction

The scaffolding practices employed in this chapter help prepare students for success in their writing. The various activities—writing a title, writing phrases with adjectives, writing sentences with appositives, and using the historical present tense—systematically build on one another in order to prepare the student to write an interesting and informative one-paragraph movie review. The following expansion activity is the final preparatory step before students write a first draft.

 EXPANSION ACTIVITY

■ Photocopy and distribute **Black Line Master 17**, "Analyzing Movie Reviews," on page BLM17 of this Teacher's Edition.

■ Put the students into small groups. Tell them that they are going to analyze and critique different movie reviews.

■ Distribute newspapers or magazines containing reviews of current movies. This activity could also be done online, if access is available. Sites like *Yahoo—Get Local*™ offer reviews on most newly released films.

■ Have students use the questions to discuss at least three different movie reviews.

■ After students have finished, have each group report to the class on the movie reviews they looked at.

8 **Writing the First Draft**

❑ Review the activity directions with the class. Discuss whether it is a good idea to include the resolution in a movie review. Ask students how they would feel if they read about the ending of a movie before they saw it.

❑ Students should write a first draft of a one-paragraph movie review, but remind them that they will revise this later. The content is the most important factor in the rough draft.

Writing with Computers

- Review the information with the class.

- Do students find having more than one document open helpful while they are writing? Are there any possible downsides, such as making changes to the wrong document? Do any of the students have any experience with splitting their screen so they can see more than one document at the same time? Do any students use alternate strategies, such as printing out different versions and comparing them?

Revising for Content and Editing for Form

1 Revising for Content

❑ Remind students that this is a revision for content, using appositives, and removing any unnecessary information. They will further edit the paragraph for form using the historical present and correcting for punctuation in Activity 4.

❑ You might have students work in pairs for this activity, then compare their answers with another pair.

❑ After students have finished, review possible changes with the class.

❑ **Note to Instructor:** The following Sample Paragraph has been revised for both content and form and should be referred to for both Activities 1 and 4.

SAMPLE PARAGRAPH

Spiderman 2: A Mild-Mannered Superhero

Spiderman 2 is the newest installment in the popular _Spiderman_ series. Actor Tobey Maguire returns as the mild-mannered Peter Parker. We see our hero having problems juggling his dual life as a college student and a superhuman crime fighter. His girlfriend, Mary Jane Watson, played by Kirsten Dunst, has found a new love. Peter considers giving up crime fighting in order to win her back, but his plans are upset when he meets his old enemy, the many-armed maniac Otto Octavius, played by Alfred Molina. Will Spiderman leave his superhero life or will he accept his fate and lose Mary Jane forever? Go see this entertaining movie and find out.

USING TWO OR MORE ADJECTIVES

■ Review the information about using two or more adjectives with the class.

■ Elicit additional examples of using more than one adjective, separated by commas, before a noun: _Nicole Kidman is a glamorous, talented actress_.

■ Elicit additional examples of using _but_ to separate two contrasting adjectives: _Willy Wonka is the story of a strange but kind man_.

2 Punctuating Sentences with Adjectives

❑ Review the activity directions and first example with the class.

❑ After students have finished, review answers with the class.

ANSWER KEY

1. _Chicago_ is an entertaining, energetic musical.
2. In _It's a Wonderful Life_, James Stewart plays a friendly, hard-working man.
3. _Cold Mountain_ is a sad, disturbing movie.
4. Spiderman is a compassionate, mild-mannered superhero.

3 Adding _But_ to Sentences with Adjectives

❑ Review the activity directions and first example with the class.

❑ After students have finished, review answers with the class.

ANSWER KEY

1. _The Aviator_ is the story of a wealthy but eccentric genius.
2. _Frankenstein_ is the story of a destructive but tragic monster.
3. _The Godfather_ is about an evil but loyal man.
4. _Million-Dollar Baby_ tells the story of a poor but determined young woman.

4 Editing for Form

- ❏ Review the activity directions with the class.

- ❏ Remind students that they are editing for verb tense and punctuation now. Students should also edit for any issues of form they've learned up to this point.

- ❏ After students have finished, review answers with the class.

- ❏ **Note to Instructor:** The Sample Paragraph following Activity 1 has been revised for both content and form and should be referred to for both Activities 1 and 4.

Evaluating Your Writing

5 Using a Rubric

Best Practice

Cultivating Critical Thinking

This activity requires students to critically evaluate their movie reviews based on both specific criteria and more general guidelines. In the following activity, students conference with a partner to compare their paragraphs and make judgments and suggestions about the overall quality of the writing.

- ❏ Review the rubric with your class. Using the completed sample paragraph from Activity 4, ask volunteers to evaluate it based on the first criteria: *Content – Paragraph describes a favorite movie so that the reader has a clear idea of the story. Paragraph contains elements of a movie review.*

- ❏ Then have students use the rubric to evaluate the movie review they wrote.

6 Peer Sharing

Best Practice

Interacting with Others

Activities such as this give students the opportunity to interact with a partner and receive constructive feedback on their writing. Here, students share their movie reviews with a partner, who compares it with his or her own writing and evaluates it according to the rubric. The expansion activity that follows gives students the chance to get an editing perspective from a peer. Students also have the chance to interact with a partner and discuss their movie-going habits in the last activity in this section.

- ❏ Note the pair icon. Give students time to exchange paragraphs and read each other's work.

- ❏ Students should discuss how well the paragraphs work according to the criteria in the rubric.

- ❏ Have students share the parts they found effective in each other's reviews with the class.

EXPANSION ACTIVITY

- ■ As a follow-up to Activity 4, have students edit each other's movie reviews for both content and form. Tell students to make notes on a separate piece of paper rather than write over their partner's work.

- ■ Pairs should then discuss the edits they made and how these improve—or don't improve—the writing.

- ■ You might walk around the class during the peer conference part of this activity, briefly discussing with each pair of students their edits and possible changes. Did students find their partner's edits useful? Did students find the process of editing their partner's work useful?

7 **Writing the Second Draft**

- ❏ Have students rewrite their paragraphs based on their own rubric evaluations from Activity 5, their peer conferences in Activity 6, and what they've learned in this chapter.

- ❏ Collect student paragraphs and make comments and corrections.

- ❏ Return students' paragraphs, then circulate through the classroom, discussing students' work and your feedback.

Focus on Testing

The Historical Present Tense

- ■ Review the TOEFL® iBT information and examples with the class.

- ■ Make sure students understand that they should use the historical present tense on the TOEFL® iBT whenever the subject of a verb refers to the lecture, the reading, the lecturer, or the author.

- ■ Ask students why this part of the test is called the "integrated" task. Elicit that the writing prompts are integrated, or connected to, information from a reading and a lecture.

Practice

- ■ Review the activity directions with the class.

- ■ Ask students if they noticed the clear references to "the lecture" and "the reading" in the prompt. Emphasize to the students that it is very important to read all TOEFL®iBT directions very carefully because they contain valuable information about completing the task.

- ■ After students have finished, review answers with the class. For each answer, ask students why they did or did not use the historical present. For example, *The subject of the verb was "the reading," so I used the historical present tense.*

- ■ For items 8 and 10 be sure to point out that "the speaker" and "he" are just other ways of saying "the lecturer."

ANSWER KEY

1. says 2. were 3. adds 4. lost 5. claims 6. were 7. notes 8. points out 9. sit 10. points to 11. was 12. cut

What Do You Think?

Analyzing How You Choose Movies

- ■ Note the pair icon. Review the directions for each section of the activity with the class. To begin the activity, you might want to talk about what is most important to you in choosing a movie and give examples. For example, *Steven Spielberg is my favorite director, and I will automatically see any film that he makes.* Make sure students are clear on the meaning of *director*, *special effects*, and any other new terms.

- ■ After students have written in their journals, ask volunteers to share any lessons they might have learned about their own movie-going habits.

Best Practice

Making Use of Academic Content

Activities such as these contain authentic materials that lead to discussions of real-world issues. Students discuss real movies and look at genuine movie reviews. In addition, the expansion activity after Activity 4 raises many controversial issues for discussion.

1   Sharing Your Writing

❑ Note the group icon. After everyone in each group has read each others' work, have the students choose the strongest review. What is it about the chosen review that is so compelling? Have each group share their chosen review with the class by reading it aloud.

❑ Encourage students to debate the merits of a film whenever different opinions arise. When students have seen the same film, have them discuss which actors gave the strongest and weakest performances. Could anything have improved the film? This discussion could be broadened to the entire class when the film has been seen by most of the students.

2   Discussing Movies

❑ To begin the activity, talk about a film that you didn't enjoy and give your reasons. For example, *I really didn't like* Crash *because of the violence*. Ask the students if anyone else has seen that film. Do they agree or disagree with your assessment?

❑ After each group has finished its discussion, have volunteers share their reasons for not liking certain movies. This could lead to a lively class discussion on those elements students do not like.

3   Writing in Your Journal

❑ The topics in the Student Book can be used as prompts for journal writing, but students can also generate their own ideas related to the theme and content of the chapter (such as *why classic films are better than modern films*).

4   Looking Up Movie Reviews

❑ Ideally this activity should be done using the Internet. If Internet access is not available to the students, have them use the library, newspapers, or other sources of movie reviews.

❑ Have students share the information they gathered with their classmates and comment on how their own review compared with others they saw.

EXPANSION ACTIVITY

■ Put the American movie ratings system on the board:

G — General audience — All ages admitted.

PG — Parental guidance suggested — Some material may not be suitable for young children.

PG-13 — Parents strongly cautioned — Some material may be inappropriate for children under 13.

R — Restricted — Under 17 requires accompanying parent or adult guardian.

NC-17 — No children 17 and under admitted.

■ Ask students if there is a similar rating system in their native countries. Do they agree with having a rating system? What movie elements should determine how a film is rated? Who should make these decisions? Have they ever been denied entry to a film they wanted to see?

Self-Assessment Log

❑ Review the statements in the self-assessment log and then have students complete it.

9

Social Life

Chapter Opener

❏ Point out the title of this chapter, "Social Life." Ask students to discuss what *social life* means to them and to make predictions about what this chapter's theme is likely to be.

❏ Have students look at the photo. Explain that these people are enjoying themselves with a group of friends. Ask students to describe ways in which they socialize with their friends. Ask and answer the questions in Connecting to the Topic.

❏ Read the quotation or call on a student to read it. Ask a volunteer to define *unpopular* and use it in a sentence. Share some of the content information about Adlai Stevenson, Jr. with students. Then ask them if they agree or disagree with the statement. Ask students what might make someone be unpopular and if a "free society" should protect them.

❏ Have students look at the description of the Writing Product. Tell them that as they work through the chapter, they should keep in mind that this will be the major writing assignment for this chapter.

Content Note

Adlai Ewing Stevenson II was born in 1900 into a political family. He was the grandson of Vice President Adlai E. Stevenson (1893-1897). Stevenson was greatly admired for his eloquence, wit, and compassion. In 1948, he was elected governor of Illinois. He was also the Democratic candidate for President in 1952 and 1956, but lost both times to President Eisenhower. In 1960, President John F. Kennedy appointed Stevenson the U.S. ambassador to the United Nations. He died in 1965, on the steps of the United States Embassy in London.

❝ A free society is a place where it's safe to be unpopular. ❞

—Adlai Stevenson, Jr.
American diplomat and politician (1900–1965)

Chapter Overview

Writing Product

A narrative paragraph about a classmate

Writing Process

- Interview a classmate.
- Write topic and concluding sentences.
- Learn methods for ordering information in a paragraph.
- Learn to use the correct verb tense.
- Use transition words and phrases: *also, in addition, in fact, however.*
- Express cause and effect with *so . . . that.*
- Learn about different contractions with *'s.*
- Spell present and past participles.
- Use correct capitalization.

Part 1: Before You Write

Exploring Ideas
Building Vocabulary
Writing Topic Sentences

Part 2: Developing Writing Skills

Using the Correct Verb Tense
Using Transition Words and Phrases
Using *In Fact*
Using *So...That*
Writing the First Draft

Part 3: Revising and Editing

Revising for Content
Editing for Form
Evaluating Your Writing
Peer Sharing
Writing the Second Draft
Focus on Testing

Part 4: Expansion Activities

Writing and Researching
Journal Writing
What Do You Think?
Self-Assessment Log

Exploring Ideas

Best Practice

Making Use of Academic Content

These activities contain authentic material that leads to discussions of real-world issues as students prepare to interview one another about their lives. Students work in groups to identify interesting interview topics, write interview questions, prepare to be interviewed themselves and interview a classmate. Students will ultimately use their own authentic material to write a narrative paragraph about their classmates.

1 Discussing Interview Topics

- ❑ Note the group icon. Before students do the activity, preview the interview that will come later in the chapter by asking students what their hobbies are.

- ❑ After students have finished working in their small groups, ask volunteers to share their answers with the class. Make a list of interview topics on the board.

ANSWER KEY

Answers may vary. Possible answers:

hobbies, work, studies, family, relationships, travel, purchases, accomplishments, disappointments.

2 Writing Interview Questions

- ❑ Model this activity for the students by writing possible questions to go with the example topic from Activity 1 on the board. Remind students to ask questions that will encourage someone to speak, as opposed to giving simple yes/no answers: *What are your hobbies? What do you like about your hobbies?* After students have finished, ask volunteers to write possible interview questions on the board. Allow other students to comment and ask questions before you make any corrections.

ANSWER KEY

Answers may vary. Possible answers:

What job did you have during the past year? What classes have you taken in the last 12 months? What new friendships or romances did you start in the past year? What trips did you take? What significant purchases did you make? What was your biggest accomplishment? What was your biggest disappointment?

3 Preparing to Be Interviewed

- ❑ Review the activity directions with the class. Encourage students to use the topics generated in the previous two activities as well as anything else that was important in their lives.

- ❑ After students have finished, ask volunteers to share any new interview topics that they generated when thinking about their own lives. Write any new topics on the board and have students ask interview questions aloud about the new topics.

- ❑ Some students may not want to talk about certain aspects of their private lives for a variety of reasons. Students' privacy should be respected.

4 Interviewing a Classmate

Best Practice

Interacting with Others

Activities such as this give students the opportunity to interact with a partner and gather authentic interview information for their writing assignment. Practicing their interviewing skills enables them to conduct a more effective interview later in the chapter.

- ❑ Note the pair icon. Review the activity directions with the class.

❑ Give students about 15 minutes to conduct their interviews. Encourage students to take good notes during the interview. They will need these notes to complete the writing project.

Building Vocabulary

5 Completing Sentences

❑ Review the activity directions with the class.

❑ After students have finished, ask volunteers to share their answers.

ANSWER KEY

Answers may vary. Possible answers:

1. Gardening 2. loves 3. classes 4. fun 5. sailing
6. enjoys 7. singing 8. tried 9. club 10. projects

REPRODUCIBLE   EXPANSION ACTIVITY

■ Photocopy and distribute **Black Line Master 18**, "Using a Vocabulary Chart," on page BLM18 of this Teacher's Edition.

■ Tell students that they are going to use a vocabulary chart very similar to the ones from previous chapters, but with one additional category: *Other*.

■ Divide students into pairs or small groups. Have them look at all of the non-underlined language in the ten sentences from Activity 5 and add as many words to the chart as they can. The first example is done for them.

■ Tell students that if they cannot determine if a word is a noun, verb, or adjective, they should place it in the *Other* category.

■ While students are working on the activity, make four columns on the board: *Nouns*, *Verbs*, *Adjectives*, and *Other*.

■ After students have finished, ask volunteers to share their answers and write the words in the appropriate column on the board. Allow students to ask questions about meanings or parts of speech.

■ A follow up to this activity would be to identify the parts of speech listed in the *Other* category.

6 Adding Suffixes

❑ Review the activity directions and first example with the class. Remind students that suffixes are always added to the end of a word.

❑ Elicit additional examples of any verbs + suffix *-ment* = *noun*: excitement, retirement, amusement.

❑ After students have finished, review answers with the class. As a follow up, you can elicit more examples with the other suffix used in the answers.

ANSWER KEY

accomplish (verb) + *-ment* = *accomplishment* (noun); *responsible* (adjective) + *-ity* = *responsibility* (noun); *difficult* (adjective) + *-y* = *difficulty* (noun)

Writing a Topic Sentence

Strategy

Writing a Topic Sentence

■ Review the information about writing a topic sentence with the class.

■ Remind students that a good topic sentence strikes a balance between being too general and too specific.

Best Practice

Scaffolding Instruction

The scaffolding practices employed in this chapter help prepare students for success in their writing. The various activities—writing a topic sentence, ordering ideas in a paragraph, writing a concluding sentence, practicing verb tenses, and using transition words and phrases—systematically build on one another in order to prepare the student to write an accurate and interesting narrative paragraph about a classmate. The expansion activity after Activity 6 in Part 2 is the final preparatory step before students write a first draft.

7 Choosing the Best Topic Sentences

❏ Review the activity directions with the class.

❏ Remind students that a topic sentence is the most general sentence in the paragraph and that it should also create reader interest in the rest of the paragraph.

❏ After the students have compared and discussed their choices with a partner, ask for volunteers to answer and explain why they chose that sentence.

ANSWER KEY

Sentences 1, 3, and 6 are the best examples of topic sentences because they are general and set the context for a detailed discussion.

8 Writing a Draft Topic Sentence

❏ You might walk around the class during this activity, briefly discussing with each pair of students their choices. Do their topic sentences capture the main idea of the information they have gathered about their partner? Would someone be interested in reading more after reading the topic sentence? Was the sentence written in the present perfect or present perfect continuous tense?

❏ After the students have discussed their sentences with the person they interviewed, ask pairs of students to comment on what they did or didn't like about their partner's topic sentence.

Strategy

Organizing Information in a Paragraph

■ Review the information about organizing information in a paragraph with the class.

■ Make sure the students understand that these are only some of the possibilities for organizing their paragraphs. Encourage students to use other ideas if they have them.

■ You might want to outline a very brief paragraph about your own activities during the past year to demonstrate one kind of organizational strategy.

9 Discussing Order of Ideas

❏ Note the group icon. Review the activity directions with the class.

❏ Remind students that there is no right or wrong way to organize a paragraph. It is up to the writer to determine which organizational strategy to use.

❏ You might walk around the class during this activity, briefly discussing with each group how they are organizing the notes.

❏ After the groups have finished, ask one student from each group to explain their strategy and then read the notes in the order they determined worked best. Note that even with just one method of organization—chronological order—there are many different starting points for the notes.

ANSWER KEY

Answers may vary. Possible answers:

Chronological Order

got married in June

went to Miami for his honeymoon

played soccer with friends in the fall

practiced soccer almost every day

read biographies in the winter

started playing chess in January

had a surprise party for his parents' anniversary in March

they have been married for 25 years

went biking with his wife in the spring

10 Ordering Ideas for Your Paragraph

❏ Review the activity directions with the class.

❏ Have pairs of students exchange notes for their paragraphs and discuss the order of ideas. Partners should give each other suggestions about how to improve the flow of ideas, where appropriate.

WRITING A CONCLUDING SENTENCE

▪ Review the information about writing a concluding sentence with the class. Make sure students understand the meaning of *wrap up*.

▪ Ask volunteers to think of a good concluding sentence for their own life during the past year. This should be a spontaneous activity that you can model for the students. For example, *The past year hasn't been the best year of my life, but I'm optimistic about the future.*

11 Identifying a Poor Concluding Sentence

❏ Review the activity directions with the class. Remind students that a poor concluding sentence doesn't wrap up, summarize, or look to the future. It introduces information that should either be elsewhere in the paragraph or eliminated.

❏ After the students have finished, ask for volunteers to share their answers with the class and explain which sentence does not make a good concluding sentence.

ANSWER KEY

The fourth sentence is a poor concluding sentence because it introduces a new topic.

12 Writing a Draft Concluding Sentence

❏ After the students have finished, you might have pairs of students exchange concluding sentences for their paragraphs and discuss them. Partners could give each other suggestions about how to improve the concluding sentence, where appropriate.

❏ Ask volunteers to share their sentences and invite students to give feedback on why these might or might not be good concluding sentences.

Developing Cohesion and Clarity

Best Practice

Cultivating Critical Thinking

The activities in this part of the chapter teach important critical thinking skills and provide varied opportunities for practicing them. Students are asked to choose the correct verb tense, identify transitional words and phrases, write new sentences, and finally, use their new skills to write a first draft of a narrative paragraph about a classmate.

USING THE CORRECT VERB TENSE

- Review the Verb Tenses chart with the class.

- Elicit additional examples of simple present tense sentences from the students: *Raed lives with his family in Cairo, Egypt.*

- Elicit additional examples of present continuous tense sentences from the students: *Raed is studying English in the evening.*

- Elicit additional examples of future tense sentences from the students: *Raed will study in Sydney, Australia, after he finishes high school.*

- Elicit additional examples of simple past tense sentences from the students: *Raed started his English classes two years ago.*

- Elicit additional examples of present perfect tense sentences from the students: *Raed has studied English for two years.*

- Elicit additional examples of present perfect continuous tense sentences from the students: *Raed has been watching English language films for several years.*

- Ask students if they find some of these verb tenses more problematic than others. Allow students to comment and ask questions on the subject.

1 **Choosing the Correct Verb Tense**

- ❑ Review the activity directions and first example with the class. Ask the students if they can give you an answer for the first example using a contraction: *He's been going to the University...* Tell students that they should refer to the verb tense chart in the previous activity if they have problems.

- ❑ After students have finished, ask volunteers to share their answers. Be prepared to discuss any sentences that seem especially problematic for the students.

ANSWER KEY

1. has been going/'s been going 2. has worked/has been working 3. joined 4. been working 5. was not/wasn't 6. was 7. tried out for 8. made 9. had 10. began 11. has played/has been playing 12. spent 13. visited 14. attended 15. had/has had

USING TRANSITION WORDS AND PHRASES: *HOWEVER, IN ADDITION, AND ALSO*

- Review the information about transition words and phrases with the class.

- Model and elicit additional examples of sentences using *however*. For example, you could model: *Raed was extremely busy with school and work last year. However, he did find time to join a band and learn to play tennis.*

- Model and elicit additional examples of sentences using *in addition*. For example, you could model: *Raed joined a band last year. In addition, he learned to play tennis.*

- Model and elicit additional examples of sentences using *also*. For example, you could model: *Raed visited his grandparents at least three times a month last year. He also attended many family gatherings.*

2 Identifying Transition Words and Phrases

❏ Review the activity directions with the class.

❏ You might have students work in pairs for this activity and then compare their answers with another pair.

❏ After students have finished, ask volunteers to identify the sentences with *however*, *in addition*, and *also*.

❏ Ask volunteers to give answers to the four questions and read the corresponding sentences aloud.

ANSWER KEY

1. in addition, also 2. however 3. at the beginning 4. Yes. *Music, however, was not Raed's only leisure time activity last year.*

USING *IN FACT*

■ Review the information about using *in fact* with the class.

■ Elicit additional examples of sentences using *in fact* from the students: *Fatima is an excellent student. In fact, she's the best student in the class.*

---

3 Rewriting Sentences with *In Fact* and *However*

❏ Review the activity directions and example with the class.

❏ Remind students that *however* is used to contrast information and *in fact* is used to support an idea or statement.

❏ After students have finished, review possible answers with the class. Note that some variations in answers are possible.

ANSWER KEY
Answers may vary. Possible answers:

1. Raed has been working very hard. In fact, he works from 8:00 in the morning until 9:00 at night.

2. Raed has been working very hard. However, he still finds time to play soccer every week./He still finds time, however, to play soccer every week.

3. Raúl has been doing well, and he likes English class a lot. However, he's been studying so much that he isn't sleeping well./He's been studying so much, however, that he isn't sleeping well./In fact, he's been studying so much that he isn't sleeping well.

4. Patricia enjoys going to school. However, she doesn't like going at night./She doesn't like going at night, however.

5. Patricia has been exercising a lot. In fact, she now runs about 30 miles a week.

4 Using Transition Words and Phrases in Sentences

❏ Review the activity directions with the class.

❏ Remind students that *however* is used to contrast information, *in fact* is used to support an idea or statement, and *also* and *in addition* are used to add information.

- ❑ You might have students finish their sentences, then compare their sentences with another student.

- ❑ Ask volunteers to share some of their sentences. Write some of the best examples on the board.

USING *SO...THAT*

- ■ Review the information about using *so...that* with the class.

- ■ Elicit additional examples of using *so...that* to show cause and effect from the students: *Ali was <u>so</u> tired yesterday <u>that</u> he fell asleep in class.*

5 Combining Sentences with *So...That*

- ❑ Review the activity directions and first example with the class.

- ❑ Ask students to identify the cause and effect in the example sentence: Cause = *Jane has been so busy*; Effect = *that she hasn't had much time to socialize*.

- ❑ After students have finished, have volunteers read their combined sentences aloud and then identify what is the cause and effect in each sentence. Allow other students to comment before you make any corrections.

ANSWER KEY

1. Jane has been so busy that she hasn't had much time to socialize. 2. Reiko was so happy that she cried. 3. Chi Wang has been working so hard that he falls asleep in class. 4. Nick has been so happy here that he is seldom homesick. 5. Sonia's daughter was so sick that she had to take her to the hospital.

6 Writing Sentences with *So...That*

- ❑ Review the activity directions with the class. Model an example for the students by writing a sentence on the board about yourself. Read the sentence aloud and identify the cause and effect. For example, *I was so late this morning that I almost forgot my books*.

- ❑ Remind students to refer to their interview notes to write the sentences.

- ❑ After students have finished, ask volunteers to share some of their sentences. Write examples on the board.

EXPANSION ACTIVITY

- Photocopy and distribute **Black Line Master 19**, "Using Transition Words and Phrases," on page BLM19 of this Teacher's Edition.

- Tell students that they are going to rewrite a paragraph by incorporating the transition words and phrases they have practiced in this chapter.

- Remind students that *however* is used to contrast information, *in fact* is used to support an idea or statement, *also* and *in addition* are used to add information, and *so...that* is used to show cause and effect.

- After students have finished, have them exchange paragraphs with another student and read each other's work. Students should compare the changes they made and discuss how well the paragraphs work using the transition words and phrases.

- Write a sample revised paragraph on the board and ask students to compare it with their own work. Allow students to comment, ask questions, and identify any different changes they made.

7 Writing the First Draft

❑ Review the activity directions with the class. Remind students of the transition words and phrases they have practiced in this chapter: *however*, *in fact*, *also*, *in addition*, and *so...that*.

❑ Students should write a first draft of a narrative paragraph about a classmate based on their interview with that person. Remind students that they will revise their paragraphs later. The content is the most important factor in the rough draft.

Revising for Content and Editing for Form

1 Revising for Content

- ❑ Note the pair icon. Have pairs of students use the questions to discuss and then revise the paragraph.

- ❑ Remind students that this is a revision for content so they should focus on organization, deleting unnecessary information, using transition words and phrases, and writing a good concluding sentence. They will further edit the paragraph for form—focusing on correct verb tense, punctuation, and capitalization—in Activity 5.

- ❑ You might have students compare their answers with those of another pair of students.

- ❑ After students have finished, review possible changes with the class.

- ❑ **Note to Instructor:** The following Sample Paragraph has been revised for both content and form and should be referred to for both Activities 1 and 5.

SAMPLE PARAGRAPH

A Great Year for Marta

Marta Duarte has had a very interesting year. Last June, she graduated from a tourism development course in Mexico. She received a scholarship to study English and has been attending classes here at the University of Ottawa since September. Marta travels throughout Canada and the United States. She visits hotels to study the different management systems and has learned a lot. In fact, she says that one day in a hotel is better than ten days in a classroom. However, Marta hasn't spent all her time in Canada working. She loves to dance and goes dancing at least two nights a week. She has also found time to develop a close friendship with the manager of a big hotel here in Ottawa. She is hoping to get to know him better.

USING CONTRACTIONS WITH 'S

- ■ Review the information about contractions with 's with the class.

- ■ Elicit additional examples of a contraction of subject + *be*: *Karen's coming.* (Karen is coming.)

- ■ Elicit additional examples of a contraction of subject + *has*: *He's been here before.* (He has been here before.)

2 Identifying 's Contractions

- ❑ Review the activity directions and first example with the class. What verb tense is the example sentence? (the simple present)

- ❑ After students have finished, review answers with the class. Ask students to identify the verb tense of each sentence.

ANSWER KEY

1. He is very satisfied with his life. (simple present) 2. She has moved three times this year. (present perfect) 3. It has been cold and rainy. (present perfect) 4. Recently she has been planning a party. (present perfect continuous) 5. It is difficult work. (simple present) 6. She has been getting dates from a computer dating service. (present perfect continuous)

3 Spelling Present and Past Participles Correctly

- ❑ Review the activity directions and first example with the class.

- ❑ Remind students that the present participle is formed by adding *-ing* to the base of a verb: *study + -ing = studying*. Also remind them that present participles indicate an uncompleted action, such as *I am reading* or *I was reading*.

- ❑ Remind students that the past participle of regular verbs is formed by adding *-ed* to the base of a verb: *work + ed = worked*. It is used for all perfect forms of the verb, such as *I have worked* and *I had worked*.

❑ After students have finished, review answers with the class.

ANSWER KEY

1. work—working/worked 2. begin—beginning/begun 3. study—studying/studied 4. make—making/made 5. find—finding/found 6. swim—swimming/swum 7. go—going/gone 8. travel—traveling/traveled 9. come—coming/come 10. have—having/had

USING CORRECT CAPITALIZATION

■ Review the guidelines for correct capitalization with the class.

■ Elicit additional examples of months and days of the week: *August*, *Wednesday*.

■ Elicit additional examples of schools and businesses: *Harvard University*, *Microsoft*.

■ Elicit additional examples of languages: *Chinese*, *English*.

4 Capitalizing Words in a Sentence

❑ Review the activity directions and first example with the class.

❑ After students have finished, review answers with the class.

❑ Ask students to compare the rules for capitalization in English with those for their native languages. Are people's names always capitalized in their native language? Are place names?

❑ After students have finished, review answers with the class.

ANSWER KEY

1. Pablo has been studying computer science and English at Northwestern College since January.
2. Anna works as a dietician at Randolph College.
3. In September, Van got a job as a mail clerk at a bank. 4. Tessa has been studying fashion design every Tuesday and Thursday evening. 5. Irena has been working with the Jones Plumbing Company since the fall.

5 Editing for Form

❑ Review the activity directions with the class.

❑ Remind students that they are editing for form at this point—in particular, for correct verb tense, punctuation, and capitalization. Students should also edit for any other issues of form they've learned up to this point.

❑ After students have finished, review answers with the class.

❑ **Note to Instructor:** The Sample Paragraph following Activity 1 has been revised for both content and form and should be referred to for both Activities 1 and 5.

Evaluating Your Writing

6 Using a Rubric

Best Practice

Cultivating Critical Thinking

This activity requires students to critically evaluate their narrative paragraphs based on both specific criteria and more general guidelines. In the following activity, students confer with a partner to compare their paragraphs and to make judgments and suggestions about the overall quality of the writing.

❑ Review the rubric with your class. Using the completed sample paragraph from Activity 5, ask volunteers to evaluate it based on the first criteria: **Content** – *Paragraph describes what a classmate has been doing in the last year*.

❑ Then have students use the rubric to evaluate the narrative paragraphs they wrote.

7 Peer Sharing

Best Practice

Interacting with Others

Activities such as this give students the opportunity to interact with a partner and receive constructive feedback on their writing. Here, students share their narrative paragraphs based on an interview with a partner who compares it with his or her own writing and evaluates it according to the correctness of the facts and the relevance of the information.

❑ Note the pair icon. Give students time to exchange paragraphs and read each other's work.

❑ Have students share the parts they found effective in each other's reviews with the class.

8 Writing the Second Draft

❑ Have students rewrite their paragraphs based on their own rubric evaluations from Activity 6, their peer conferences in Activity 7, and what they've learned in this chapter.

❑ Collect student paragraphs and make comments and corrections.

❑ Return students' paragraphs, then circulate through the classroom, discussing students' work and your feedback.

Writing with Computers

■ Review the information about the *undo* feature with the class.

■ Do students make use of the *undo* feature when they are writing? In which menu is the *undo* command located? Can anyone describe the *undo* icon in a word-processing program? Does anyone know a keyboard shortcut for *undo*? Are there any possible downsides, such as undoing too many steps and losing information?

Focus on Testing TOEFL® iBT

Managing Your Time on Standardized Tests

■ Review the TOEFL®iBT information and time planning strategy with the class.

■ Make sure students understand that these are just suggestions to help students prepare for the test. The actual way that students divide their time will vary.

■ Remind students that the "independent" writing task will consist of a prompt that will have them write for 30 minutes about a personal experience or personal preference. In the "integrated" task, the writing prompts are integrated, or connected to, information from a reading and a lecture.

Practice

■ Review the activity directions with the class. This activity can be done in class or assigned as homework.

■ Ask students if this is an "independent" or "integrated" writing task and to explain why.

■ After students have finished, collect student paragraphs and make comments and corrections.

1 Sharing Your Writing

❑ Note the group icon. Have students use photographs, drawings, or other materials to complement the paragraphs about them.

❑ Have students determine a title for their newsletter and for the lead article, as well as what photograph or illustration they might use. Encourage students to be as creative as possible. Allow them to determine if they prefer the paragraphs to be typed or handwritten.

❑ Pass the newsletter around the class or give it to another English class to read.

2 Guessing the Classmate

Best Practice

Activating Prior Knowledge

These activities give students the opportunity to link prior knowledge to new information they acquire through listening to, reading, and writing narrative paragraphs about classmates and famous people.

❑ Note the pair icon. Model this activity by orally giving a brief narrative about a famous person without mentioning his or her name. Tell students to raise their hands as soon as they think they know who the person is.

❑ After students have exchanged paragraphs and guessed identities, ask students to tell what information "gave away" the student's identity.

❑ Involve yourself in this activity by allowing students to pass unnamed paragraphs to you as well.

EXPANSION ACTIVITY

▪ Have students write a brief narrative about a famous person without mentioning his or her name.

▪ Remind students to employ as many of the writing strategies they practiced in this chapter as possible.

▪ After students have finished, ask volunteers to read their paragraphs aloud and let the other students guess the person's identity.

3 Writing About Your Class

❑ Note the group icon. Review the activity directions with the class. This activity can be done in class or as homework.

❑ Encourage students to write about any group of people they choose. Their English class is just one possibility.

❑ After students have finished, invite volunteers to share their writing with the class.

4 Writing in Your Journal

❑ The topic in the Student Book can be used as a prompt for journal writing, but students can also generate their own ideas related to the theme and content of the chapter (such as *what I don't like doing every day*).

What Do You Think?

Evaluating a Day in Your Life

■ Review the activity directions with the class. Ask students why this kind of graphic organizer is called a *pie chart*. For example, it can be sliced up into pieces—just like a pie.

■ After students have finished, have them share their pie charts with a partner and compare how they spend their time. Students should discuss what they would like to spend more and less time doing.

■ Students should reconvene with their partners after they have completed their ideal day pie chart. Do they have similar dreams of how to spend their time?

■ Ask volunteers to share any lessons they have learned from this activity with the class.

5 Researching a Sport or Hobby

❏ Ideally this activity should be done using the Internet. If Internet access is not available to the students, have them use the library, reference materials, or other sources of information about sports and hobbies.

❏ Have students share the information they gathered with their small group and discuss the questions.

❏ After the small groups have finished their discussions, ask students to share what they've learned with the class.

Self-Assessment Log

❏ Review the statements in the self-assessment log and then have students complete it.

10

Sports

Chapter Opener

❏ Point out the title of this chapter, "Sports." Ask students if sports are important to them, and ask them to make predictions about what this chapter's theme is likely to be.

❏ Have students look at the photo. Explain that this person is kayaking. Ask students if they have ever tried any "extreme" sports. Ask and answer the questions in Connecting to the Topic.

❏ Read the quotation or call on a student to read it. Share some of the content information about George F. Will with students. Then ask them if they agree or disagree with the statement, and ask them to support their opinions with examples. Ask students if sports ever provide vivid examples of poor behavior, as well.

❏ Have students look at the description of the Writing Product. Tell them that as they work through the chapter, they should keep in mind that this will be the major writing assignment for this chapter.

Content Note

George Frederick Will is an American political columnist who was born in Champaign, Illinois, in 1941. His editorial columns appear in the *Washington Post* newspaper and *Newsweek* magazine. He also appears regularly on television news programs. In 1977, he won a Pulitzer Prize for distinguished commentary. Will has also written books about American baseball, including *Men at Work: The Craft of Baseball* (1990) and *Bunts* (1998).

❝ Sports serve society by providing vivid examples of excellence. ❞

—George F. Will
American newspaper columnist (1941–)

Chapter Overview

Writing Product

A paragraph comparing two sports

Writing Process

- Categorize sports.
- Find bases of comparison.
- Use a Venn diagram.
- Use a comparison table.
- Write a topic sentence.
- Write a concluding sentence.
- Use comparative adjectives and adverbs.
- Use *both* to write about similarities.
- Use *but* and *however* to write about differences.

Part 1: Before You Write

Exploring Ideas
Building Vocabulary
Organizing Ideas
What Do You Think?

Part 2: Developing Writing Skills

Using Comparitives
Writing About Similarities
Writing About Differences
Writing the First Draft

Part 3: Revising and Editing

Revising for Content
Editing for Form
Evaluating Your Writing
Peer Sharing
Writing the Second Draft
Focus on Testing

Part 4: Expansion Activities

Writing and Researching
Journal Writing
Self-Assessment Log

Exploring Ideas

Best Practice

Organizing Information

The activities in the first part of the chapter will allow students to practice and build on the organizational skills they have developed in previous chapters. First, students will use a chart to categorize sports into four different categories. Next, students will use a vocabulary chart to identify word families. After that, students will create Venn diagrams to map out the similarities and differences between the two sports they have chosen to write about. Finally, students will use the information in their Venn diagrams to establish bases of comparison for their paragraph in a comparison table. Working with tools such as these helps students organize information for their writing in a variety of different ways.

1 Categorizing Sports

❏ Note the group icon. Before students do the activity, have them use their dictionaries to find the meaning of any unfamiliar sports. Discuss the meanings as a class. It is likely that they will not know some of the more obscure sports' names.

❏ While students are working in small groups, make a chart on the board with the four sports categories.

❏ After students have finished working in their small groups, ask volunteers to share their answers with the class. List their answers on the board, making note of those sports that can be listed in more than one category. Let the students discuss any disagreements over placing sports in particular categories.

ANSWER KEY

Answers may vary. Possible answers:

Winter	Dangerous	Water	Team
ice hockey	fencing	kite surfing	baseball
ice skating	horseback riding	scuba diving	basketball
skiing	ice hockey	swimming	bowling
snowboarding	karate	water skiing	ice hockey
	kite surfing	windsurfing	soccer
	rock climbing		tennis
	scuba diving		volleyball
	skiing		
	snowboarding		
	water skiing		
	ice hockey		
	windsurfing		

❑ Ask volunteers to share any other categories that they think would be useful for categorizing sports and give examples of the sports in those categories.

2 Choosing a Topic

❑ Encourage students to choose two sports or types of sports that they think will be interesting for others to read about.

❑ After students have finished, ask students to share their choices and explain why they think it would be an interesting comparison. Allow other students to comment and ask questions.

Building Vocabulary

3 Using a Vocabulary Chart

❑ Note the group icon. Review the activity directions and chart categories with the class.

❑ While students are working in their groups, make three columns on the board: *Nouns*, *Verbs*, and *Adjectives*.

❑ After students have finished, ask volunteers to share their answers and write any new words in the appropriate column on the board. Allow students to ask questions about meaning or parts of speech.

ANSWER KEY

Answers may vary. Possible answers:

Nouns: referee, stadium, endorsement

Verbs: replay, strategize, recover

Adjectives: professional, amateur, active

WORD FAMILIES

■ Review the information about word families with the class.

■ Elicit additional examples of any word families the students can think of, such as *student*, *study*, and *studious*.

4 Finding Word Families

❑ Review the activity directions and first examples with the class.

❑ After students have finished, ask volunteers to share their answers with the class. Make a list of the word families on the board. Ask students to state the part of speech of each word and its meaning.

ANSWER KEY

Answers may vary. Possible answers:

Note to Instructor: These possible answers do not include any additions to the list that students might make.

competition, compete, competitive, competitor

danger, dangerous

energy, energetic

individual, individual

loser, lose

opponent, oppose, opposing

participant, participate

race, race

score, score

talent, talented

winner, win, winning

 EXPANSION ACTIVITY

■ Photocopy and distribute **Black Line Master 20**, "Word Families," on page BLM20 of this Teacher's Edition.

■ Tell students that they are going to continue identifying word families from vocabulary they have seen in previous chapters.

■ Divide students into pairs or small groups. Have them write as many words for each word listed as possible.

■ Remind students that word families are groups of words that have similar meanings but usually have different forms for different parts of speech. Forms can sometimes be the same for different parts of speech; for example, *race* (noun), *race* (verb).

■ Tell students that they should be prepared to identify the different parts of speech as well as the meanings of the new words.

Organizing Ideas

Best Practice

Scaffolding Instruction

The scaffolding practices employed in this chapter help prepare students for success in their writing. The various activities—creating a Venn diagram, discussing bases of comparison, writing a draft topic sentence, writing a draft concluding sentence, using comparatives, writing about similarities using *both*, and writing about differences using *but* and *however*—systematically build on one another in order to prepare the student to write an interesting paragraph comparing two sports or types of sports.

Strategy

Using Venn Diagrams

■ Review the information on Venn diagrams with the class.

■ Draw the following diagram on the board.

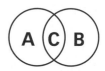

■ Ask students what letters would show the similarities and differences between two sports or other things. Elicit that letter C would show the similarities between two things and letters A and B would show the differences.

5 **Using a Venn Diagram**

❑ Review the activity directions with the class. Discuss the first phrase, *played any time of year*, with the class. Allow students to come up with the best answer: *basketball*. **Note to instructor:** These answers may vary according to where you are in the world. For example, in a warm climate, baseball could, in fact, be played any time of year.

❑ You might choose to have the students work in pairs to complete this activity. While students are working, draw a large Venn diagram for basketball and baseball on the board.

❑ After the students have finished, ask for volunteers to give their answers and reasoning. Allow for discussion before you place each phrase in the appropriate space.

ANSWER KEY

Basketball: played any time of year, fast, played inside, use ball and net

Baseball: played only in good weather, played outside, use gloves and bat, slow

Both: played with a ball, team sport

6 Creating a Venn Diagram

❑ Make sure the students are clear on what their task is: they need to first choose the two sports they will compare, then write the similarities in the overlapping parts of the circles, and the differences in the parts that do not overlap.

❑ While students are filling in their diagrams, walk around the class and discuss how similar or different each student's two sports are.

❑ Ask volunteers to share what they learned from diagramming their two sports. Will they be writing more about the similarities or the differences? Why?

What Do You Think?

Finding Interesting Bases of Comparison

■ Review the information about bases of comparison with the class.

■ Remind students that whether they focus on similarities or differences, they should try to find bases of comparison that others will find unusual or interesting.

Discussing Bases of Comparison

■ Note the group icon. Review the activity directions and make sure the class is clear on the meanings of the different sports.

■ Encourage students to think of what would be most interesting for others to read about. After the groups have finished, broaden the discussion to include the entire class.

■ Ask volunteers to share what they would concentrate on and explain why. Allow other students to comment and ask questions.

7 Creating a Comparison Table

❑ Review the activity directions and sample comparison table with the class.

❑ Remind students that they can focus on either differences or similarities for their bases of comparison.

❑ While students are filling in their tables, walk around the class and discuss each student's bases of comparison. Will these be interesting to read about?

❑ You might also have students compare their tables with a partner and get feedback.

8 Discussing Topic Sentences

- ❑ Note the pair icon. Remind students that a topic sentence is usually the most general sentence in a paragraph and all the ideas in the paragraph should relate to it.

- ❑ Have students use the two questions to analyze the four example topic sentences.

- ❑ After students have finished, ask volunteers to share their analyses with the class. Ask students what they think is the most interesting topic sentence and to explain why.

ANSWER KEY

1. swimming and diving/differences
2. windsurfing and water skiing/similarities
3. American football and World Cup football/ differences 4. team sports and individual sports/ differences

9 Writing a Draft Topic Sentence

- ❑ You might walk around the class during this activity, briefly discussing with each student his or her sentence. Does the topic sentence make clear which two sports will be discussed? Does the topic sentence make clear whether the similarities or the differences between the two sports will be discussed? Would someone be interested in reading more after reading the topic sentence?

- ❑ After the students have finished, ask volunteers to share their topic sentences with the class. Allow other students to comment and ask questions.

WRITING A CONCLUDING SENTENCE

- ▪ Review the information about writing a concluding sentence with the class.

- ▪ Remind students that a good concluding sentence wraps up or summarizes the paragraph.

- ▪ Model and elicit additional examples of concluding sentences using *In my opinion*: *In my opinion, American football shouldn't be called* football *at all*.

- ▪ Model and elicit additional examples of concluding sentences using *To my mind*: *To my mind, extreme sports like snowboarding are the future of the Olympics.*

- ▪ Model and elicit additional examples of concluding sentences using *If you ask me*: *If you ask me, golf is a boring sport.*

10 Writing a Draft Concluding Sentence

- ❑ After the students have finished, you might have pairs of students exchange concluding sentences for their paragraphs. Partners could give each other suggestions to improve the concluding sentence when appropriate.

- ❑ Ask volunteers to share their sentences and invite students to give feedback on why these would or would not be good concluding sentences.

Developing Cohesion and Clarity

Best Practice

Cultivating Critical Thinking

The activities in this part of the chapter teach important critical thinking skills and provide varied opportunities for practicing them. Students are asked to recognize the comparative forms of adjectives and adverbs, use *both* before nouns, adjectives, verbs, and as a pronoun, and use *but* and *however* to write about differences. Students then synthesize all of this new information and incorporate it in a first draft of a paragraph comparing two sports.

USING COMPARATIVES

- Review the information about adjectives, spelling notes, and adverbs with the class. Make sure students understand the meaning of *syllable*. You might want to model and then have students sound out some words; for example, *ex-pen-sive*.

- Elicit additional examples of comparing with one-syllable adjectives with *-er + than*: *Egypt is hotter than Canada*.

- Elicit additional examples of comparing with two-syllable adjectives that end in *-y*: *Dogs are more friendly/friendlier than cats*.

- Elicit additional examples of comparing with adjectives of more than two syllables: *I think basketball is more exciting than baseball*.

- Elicit examples of comparing two verbs using *more*: *He runs more gracefully than he dances*.

- Elicit examples of modifying an adverb with *more*: *I wish I could learn more quickly*.

- Elicit examples of irregular adverbs with *-er*: *He needs to work a lot harder*.

- Ask students which of these comparative forms they might use often, and which they would find difficult to use. Allow students to comment and ask questions on the subject.

1 Forming Comparative Adjectives

- ❏ Review the activity directions with the class. You might want to pair weaker and stronger students to complete this activity.

- ❏ After students have finished, ask volunteers to share their answers. Be prepared to discuss any adjectives or adverbs that seem especially problematic for the students.

ANSWER KEY

1. more competitive 2. faster 3. more exciting
4. more athletic 5. more sleepy/sleepier 6. more difficult 7. fatter 8. more slowly 9. better
10. better 11. more tiring 12. more boring
13. more dangerous 14. safer 15. more aggressively

EXPANSION ACTIVITY

- As a follow up to Activity 1, have students work in pairs or small groups to create sentences using the 15 comparative forms they just completed.

- Write an example on the board for the first adjective, such as *The other team was a lot more competitive than I imagined*. Tell students that this is just an example and they should come up with their own sentence for *more competitive*.

- After the students have finished, ask volunteers to share their answers. Allow more than one student to give a sentence for each word. Write some of the best examples on the board.

WRITING ABOUT SIMILARITIES: USING *BOTH*

- Review the information and examples on using *both* with the class.

- Elicit additional examples of using *both* before nouns: *Both basketball and hockey have very fast action*.

- Elicit additional examples of using *both* before adjectives: *Horse racing and dog racing are both exciting*.

- Elicit additional examples of using *both* before verbs: *Soccer and volleyball players both use a similar size ball*.

- Elicit additional examples of using *both* as a pronoun: *Both are team sports*.

2 Combining Sentences with *Both*

- ❏ Review the activity directions and first examples with the class.

- ❏ After students have finished, have volunteers read their combined sentences aloud and then identify whether *both* occurs before a noun, adjective, or verb, or whether it is a pronoun. Allow other students to comment before you make any corrections.

ANSWER KEY

1. Both bowling and ping pong are fun.
   Bowling and ping pong are both fun.
   Both are fun.
2. Both scuba diving and skiing are expensive.
   Scuba diving and skiing are both expensive.
   Both are expensive.
3. Both baseball and football require equipment.
   Baseball and football both require equipment.
   Both require equipment.
4. Both boxing and wrestling can be dangerous.
   Boxing and wrestling can both be dangerous.
   Both can be dangerous.
5. Both skiing and snowboarding are done in the winter.
   Skiing and snowboarding are both done in the winter.
   Both are done in the winter.

6. Both competitive and team sports are on TV.
   Competitive and team sports are both on TV.
   Both are on TV.

WRITING ABOUT DIFFERENCES: USING *BUT* AND *HOWEVER*

- Review the information about using *but* and *however* to write about differences with the class.

- Elicit additional examples of using *but* to combine two parallel sentences: *Ice skating takes place on ice, but in-line skating doesn't*.

- Elicit additional examples of using *but* to combine two sentences that are not parallel: *Surfing is a dangerous sport, but fatalities are very rare*.

- Elicit additional examples of using *however* to introduce a contrasting idea: *Scuba diving can be expensive. However, it is amazing! Scuba diving can be expensive; however, it is amazing!*

- Make sure students understand what a semicolon is.

3 Rewriting Sentences with *But* and *However*

- ❏ Review the activity directions and first example with the class. Ask a volunteer to give the other variation of the first example using *however*: *Golf may be interesting to some people. However, I think it's incredibly silly*.

- ❏ After students have finished, have volunteers read their rewritten sentences aloud and identify what punctuation changes they made. With sentences that use *however* there will be two possible answers.

ANSWER KEY

1. Golf may be interesting to some people; however, I think it's incredibly silly. 2. Ice hockey can be very violent, but it's also extremely exciting to watch. 3. When I was a child, I loved to participate in sports; however, now I prefer to be a spectator. / When I was a child, I loved to participate in sports. However, now I prefer to be a spectator. 4. I love going to football games, but I always feel bad if my team loses. 5. I admire windsurfers; however, I'd be too scared to try windsurfing. / I admire windsurfers. However, I'd be too scared to try windsurfing. 6. Skiing looks like fun; however, I never go because I hate speed and I'm afraid of heights. / Skiing looks like fun. However, I never go because I hate speed and I'm afraid of heights.

4 Rewriting Sentences Using *Both*, *But*, and *However*

❑ Review the activity directions and first example with the class.

❑ Remind students that when writing about similarities, *both* can come before a noun, adjective, or verb, or can be used as a pronoun.

❑ After students have finished, have volunteers read their rewritten sentences aloud and then identify what changes they made. Did they combine the sentences? How did they use *however*—to start a new sentence or with a semicolon?

ANSWER KEY

1. Both team and individual sports are fun; however, they are different in two important ways. /Both team and individual sports are fun. However, they are different in two important ways. 2. The first difference is that you can do individual sports alone. You don't need anyone to go cycling or running, but a football player can't just pick up a ball and decide to play. 3. Volleyball and baseball both require opponents. 4. Ice skating and rock climbing both require no teammates. 5. Basketball and soccer both require teammates; however, you can practice them on your own. / Basketball and soccer both require teammates. However, you can practice them on your own.

5 Writing the First Draft

❑ Review the activity directions with the class.

❑ Students should write a first draft of a paragraph comparing two sports. Remind students that they will revise their paragraph later. The content is the most important factor in the first draft.

Writing with Computers

■ Review the information about using the highlight feature with the class.

■ Do students make use of this feature when they are writing? In which menu is the highlight feature located? Can anyone describe the highlight icon in a word-processing program? What color do students typically highlight in?

Revising for Content and Editing for Form

1 Revising for Content

❑ Review the activity directions with the class.

❑ After students have finished, ask volunteers to share their choices of the best topic sentence. Allow other students to comment and ask questions.

❑ Review possible content changes to the paragraph with the class.

❑ **Note to Instructor:** The following Sample Paragraph has been revised for both content and form and should be referred to for both Activities 1 and 2.

SAMPLE PARAGRAPH

Both team sports and individual sports are fun; however, they are different in two important ways. The first difference is that you can do individual sports alone. For example, you do not need anyone to go cycling or running. However, a tennis player can not just pick up a racket and decide to play. A tennis player needs an opponent. Team sports such as volleyball and baseball need even more people, and they both require two opposing teams and space to play. Soon you need schedules, teams, and uniforms. Team sports are much more formal than individual sports. In addition, there is another major difference between team and individual sports: the score. When I go ice skating, no one judges my performance. Similarly, there are no losers in rock climbing. But only one team in a football game is the winner, and one is the loser. Competition can make even an informal game of ping pong stressful. In my opinion, sports should be fun. However, team sports create a lot of work and a lot of stress.

2 Editing for Form

❑ Review the activity directions with the class.

❑ Remind students that they are editing for problems with connecting words and comparative structures. Students should also edit for any other issues of form they've learned up to this point.

❑ After students have finished, review answers with the class.

❑ **Note to Instructor:** The Sample Paragraph following Activity 1 has been revised for both content and form and should be referred to for both Activities 1 and 2.

Evaluating Your Writing

3 Using a Rubric

Best Practice

Cultivating Critical Thinking

This activity requires students to critically evaluate their comparative paragraphs based on both specific criteria and more general guidelines. In the following activity, students conference with a partner to compare their paragraphs and make judgments and suggestions about the overall quality of the writing.

❑ Review the rubric with your class. Using the completed sample paragraph from Activity 2, ask volunteers to evaluate it based on the first criteria: **Content** – *Paragraph compares two sports, states preference, and includes interesting bases of comparison.*

❑ Then have students use the rubric to evaluate the narrative paragraph they wrote.

4 Peer Sharing

Best Practice

Interacting with Others

Activities such as this give students the opportunity to interact with a partner and receive constructive feedback on their writing. Here, students share their comparative paragraph with a partner, who compares it with his or her own writing and evaluates it according to his or her own level of interest. Partners also give reasons as to why they agree or disagree with the opinion stated in the paragraph.

❑ Note the pair icon. Give students time to exchange paragraphs and read each other's work.

❑ Students should discuss how well the paragraphs work according to the criteria in the rubric. They should also give reasons why they agree or disagree with the author.

❑ Have students share the parts they found effective in each other's reviews with the class.

5 Writing the Second Draft

❑ Have students rewrite their paragraphs based on their own rubric evaluations from Activity 3, their peer conferences in Activity 4, and what they've learned in this chapter.

❑ Collect students' paragraphs and make comments and corrections.

❑ Return students' paragraphs, then circulate through the classroom, discussing students' work and your feedback.

Focus on Testing

Describing Differences

■ Review the TOEFL®iBT strategy on using connectors, such as *but* and *however* with the class.

■ Remind students that the "independent" writing task will consist of a prompt that will have them write for 30 minutes about a personal experience or personal preference.

Practice

■ Review the activity directions, chart, and first example with the class.

■ Make sure students understand all of the vocabulary in the chart, such as *origin*, *status*, and *dress*.

■ After students have finished, ask volunteers to share their answers with the class.

ANSWER KEY

Answers may vary. Possible answers:

1. A skier uses two narrow boards, but a snowboarder uses only a single wide one.

2. Skiing is hundreds of years old, but snowboarding began in the 1960s.

3. There is no known inventor of skiing; however, we know that snowboarding was invented by Sherman Poppen of Muskegon, Michigan.

4. In the 1970s, skiing was allowed on hills at commercial resorts, but snowboarding was not.

5. Skiers in the 1970s wore expensive, special clothing. However, snowboarders wore ordinary, inexpensive clothes.

6. There are many skiers over the age of 30, but not many snowboarders.

Best Practice

Making Use of Academic Content

This chapter abounds in content-based, authentic material. These activities contain materials that naturally lead to a discussion of real-world issues. Students work with their classmates to discuss sports and hobbies, write about and discuss Olympic sports and sports celebrities, and conduct a comparative analysis of the Olympic Games.

1 Discussing Sports and Hobbies with a Partner

- ❑ Note the pair icon. If partners cannot find a sport or hobby that is unique to them, have them switch partners.

- ❑ After students have chosen three bases of comparison and discussed how the sports or hobbies are similar or different, have them write as many sentences using *both*, *but*, and *however* as possible. Students should also use as many comparative forms of adjectives and adverbs as they can.

- ❑ Ask pairs to share their comparative sentences on their sports or hobbies with the class.

2 Writing About a Sport

Best Practice

Activating Prior Knowledge

Activities such as these give students opportunities to link prior knowledge to new information they acquire through discussion, writing, and research. In this case, students draw on their prior knowledge of a sport and use the comparative tools they have developed in this chapter to organize and present their arguments to the class.

- ❑ To begin this activity, have a brief discussion about the Olympic Games. How often are they held? Which city hosted the last Games? Do students prefer the summer or winter Games? Why? What are the students' favorite Olympic sports?

- ❑ After students have had a chance to write their paragraphs, ask volunteers to read their writing aloud to make the case for including their sports in the Olympics. Allow other students to respond. Do they agree that the sport should be included? Why or why not?

- ❑ Involve yourself in this activity by putting forward your own argument for including a sport.

3 Writing About Sports Celebrities

- ❑ Note the group icon. Begin the activity by having a discussion about celebrities in sports. Do students think that sports celebrities receive too much attention and money? Are professional sports good for society? Ask students who their favorite athlete is and why.

- ❑ After groups have had a chance to write their paragraphs, ask volunteers to read their comparisons of celebrities aloud. Allow other students to respond and ask questions.

- ❑ Involve yourself in this activity by putting forward your own comparison.

4 Writing in Your Journal

- ❑ The topics in the Student Book can be used as prompts for journal writing, but students can also generate their own ideas related to the theme and content of the chapter (such as *How the Olympic Games compare with national sports*).

5 **Researching the Olympic Games**

❑ Ideally this activity should be done using the Internet. If Internet access is not available, have students use the library, reference materials, or other sources of information about sports and the Olympic Games.

❑ You might want to have students complete this activity in pairs or small groups.

❑ After the students have finished, ask volunteers to share what they've learned with the class.

REPRODUCIBLE **EXPANSION ACTIVITY**

■ Photocopy and distribute **Black Line Master 21**, "The Ancient Olympic Games," on page BLM21 of this Teacher's Edition.

■ Tell students that they are going to write comparative sentences about the ancient Olympics versus the modern Olympics.

■ Remind students to use *both* when writing about similarities. When writing about differences, they should use *but* or *however*.

■ Have students use the information provided on the handout along with any relevant information they gathered in their research for Activity 5.

■ After students have finished, ask volunteers to read their comparative sentences aloud and let the other students comment and discuss.

■ Write some of the best comparative sentences on the board.

Self-Assessment Log

❑ Review the statements in the self-assessment log and then have students complete it.

BLM 1

Name _____ Date _____

Academic Life

Directions: Answer the questions below. Be prepared to discuss your answers with the class.

1. What are some reasons people go to universities?

_____

_____

_____

_____

2. What are some of the majors offered at universities?

_____

_____

_____

_____

3. Where do students live?

_____

_____

_____

_____

4. What do students do for fun?

_____

_____

_____

_____

5. Name some universities in your country and around the world.

_____

_____

_____

_____

BLM 2

Name _____   Date _____

Vocabulary Chart

Directions: Think of a vocabulary topic related to "Academic Life around the World." Then break that topic into vocabulary categories. List as many vocabulary items as you can think of for each category.

Topic:				
Categories				
_____	_____	_____	_____	_____
_____	_____	_____	_____	_____
_____	_____	_____	_____	_____
_____	_____	_____	_____	_____
_____	_____	_____	_____	_____
_____	_____	_____	_____	_____
_____	_____	_____	_____	_____
_____	_____	_____	_____	_____
_____	_____	_____	_____	_____
_____	_____	_____	_____	_____
_____	_____	_____	_____	_____

Name _____ Date _____

Connecting Sentences

Directions: Write new sentences below with *and*, *but*, *so*, and *also*. Pay attention to your use of commas. The first example is done for you. More than one answer is possible in some cases.

1. She needs to save some money. She is working a part-time job.

   She needs to save money, so she is working a part-time job. _____

2. He wants to watch the movie. He doesn't have any time.

   _____

3. Fouad likes classical music. He likes rock music.

   _____

4. Karen likes tomatoes. Karen likes carrots.

   _____

5. Yoshi doesn't have a notebook. He needs to buy one.

   _____

6. Catherine is married. She has two children.

   _____

7. Ali plays football on the weekend. He does homework on the weekend.

   _____

8. Tim has the CD. He can't find it.

   _____

9. I'm not feeling well. I need to see the doctor.

   _____

10. He really likes school. He really likes learning about the world.

   _____

BLM 4

Name _____ Date _____

Nature

Directions: Answer the questions below. Be prepared to discuss your answers with the class.

1. How is nature important to you? Explain.

_____

_____

_____

_____

2. What in nature do you most enjoy?

_____

_____

_____

_____

3. Does nature ever scare you? If so, give examples.

_____

_____

_____

_____

4. Do you think we are doing enough to protect nature?

_____

_____

_____

_____

5. Name some natural wonders in your country and around the world.

_____

_____

_____

_____

Name _____   Date _____

Useful Vocabulary

Directions: During your group discussion, write down any vocabulary that you might use in your writing product – the descriptive paragraph about a painting. You can also add to this chart as you complete the chapter. Put each vocabulary item in the appropriate category.

Nouns	Adjectives	Verbs	Other

Name _____   Date _____

Food

Directions: Answer the questions below. Be prepared to discuss your answers with the class.

1. What are some of your favorite foods or dishes?

_____

_____

_____

_____

2. What are some foods that you don't like? Why?

_____

_____

_____

_____

3. What is the most exotic food you have ever eaten?

_____

_____

_____

_____

4. Name at least three famous dishes from your country and three more from other countries.

_____

_____

_____

_____

5. What are some of the foods and dishes associated with different holidays in your country?

_____

_____

_____

_____

Name _____   Date _____

Useful Vocabulary

Directions: Write down any vocabulary that might be useful in your writing. Put the vocabulary item in the appropriate category. Some words may be listed in more than one category.

Nouns	Verbs	Adjectives	Other
kabobs	mix	spicy	especially

Foods that contain vegetables:

Foods that are sweet:

Foods that contain meat:
kabobs

Foods that you eat cold:

Foods that you eat hot:

BLM 8

Name _____   Date _____

How to Get to My Home

Directions: Draw a map showing how to get from your school to your home. Then give directions to your partner. Your partner should take notes and read back the directions to make sure they're correct.

 **BLM 9**

Name _____ Date _____

Mapping Information

Directions: Use the graphic organizer below to map information about the types of activities that are available at your school and in your community. Write the main topic in the large circle and details in the smaller circles. Add circles as needed.

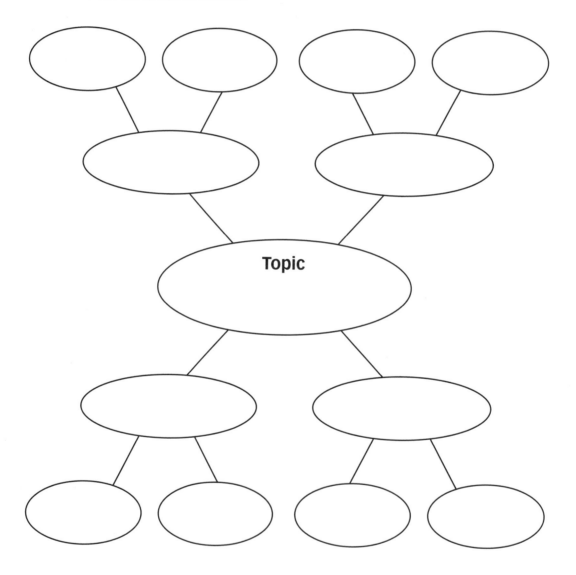

Name _____ Date _____

My Life

Directions: Fill in the boxes with information you will use to write the paragraph about your life.

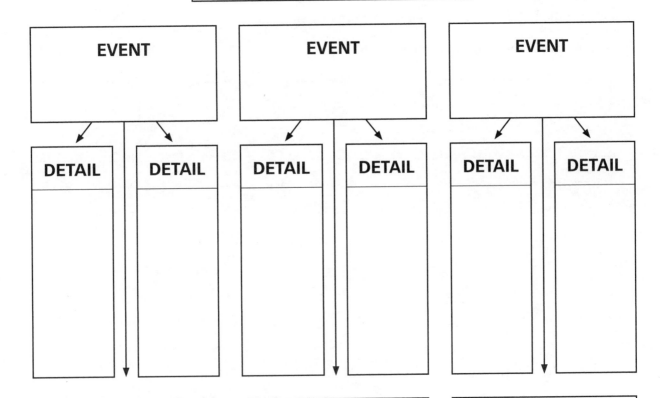

Name _____   Date _____

In the Past

Directions: Combine the sentences below with time words, conjunctions, and *because*. Pay attention to punctuation. Write as many answers for each example as you can. The first example is done for you.

1. She bought an expensive sports car. She won the lottery.

As soon as she won the lottery, she bought an expensive sports car.

She bought an expensive sports car as soon as she won the lottery.

She bought an expensive sports car because she won the lottery.

After she won the lottery, she bought an expensive sports car.

She won the lottery, so she bought an expensive sports car.

2. He moved to Riyadh. He got a job as an engineer.

_____

_____

_____

_____

_____

3. He got a big promotion at work. He asked his girlfriend to marry him.

_____

_____

_____

_____

_____

4. I was very happy. My daughter started school.

_____

_____

_____

_____

_____

5. They did a lot of research. They bought a hybrid car.

_____

_____

_____

Name _____   Date _____

Time Words

Directions: Complete the following story using the time words and phrases listed below. In some cases, more than one answer is correct, and the words can be used more than once.

> when   while   as soon as   then

_____ I was ten years old, my family went on vacation to Hawaii.

_____ we arrived, the Hawaiian girls put tropical flowers around our

necks. _____ we took a taxi to our hotel. _____

our parents were checking into the hotel, my sister and I went outside to see the ocean. Our

hotel was right on the beach. _____ we went to our rooms and put on

our bathing suits. For seven days we swam in the ocean, ate delicious food, and did lots of

fun activities. _____ we got home, we had so many great pictures to

look at. It was our best vacation ever.

Name _____ Date _____

What's the Story?

Directions: Read the story below. After you have finished reading, guess what the original story was. How are the two versions different? Is the moral the same in both versions?

Once upon a time, there was a little girl named Clara. The only thing was, Clara wasn't so little. Clara was the tallest girl in her school. In fact, she was taller than all the boys as well.

Not only was Clara very, very tall, she was also very clumsy. The other kids would make fun of her and call her names. Clara's mother tried to make her feel better, but Clara was sad most of the time.

One day, Clara and her mother went into the city to do some shopping. While the car was stopped at a red light, Clara saw a group of tall girls going into a building. "Hey, Mom, look at those girls! They look just like me," Clara said. The name above the door on the building read *City Girls Basketball*.

As soon as Clara entered the building with her mother, she knew her life would never be the same. She had found her own kind. These girls wouldn't make fun of her. In fact, they welcomed Clara. And you know what happened? In time, Clara became the best basketball player on the whole team.

Name _____ Date _____

Word Pairs

Directions: Below is a list of words from this and previous chapters. Identify what part of speech each word is, then change the word by adding one of the following suffixes: *-er*, *-ly*, *-ful*, *-ment*, and *–al*, and identify the part of speech of the new word. You can also add any examples of your own to the list.

Word	POS*	Suffix	New Word	POS
traditional	adjective	*-ly*	traditionally	adverb
thank				
mine				
selfish				
immediate				
power				
kind				
respect				
farm				
eventual				
inform				
excite				

*Part of Speech

BLM 15

Name _____ Date _____

KWL Chart

Using the Internet or the library, research a topic about either traditional or modern medicine that you would like to know more about, such as CAT scans or acupuncture. Before you begin your research, list details in the first two columns. Fill in the last column after completing your research.

What I Know	What I Want to Know	What I Learned

BLM 16

Name _____   Date _____

Adjectives

Directions: Work in small groups. Look at the list of famous movies and actors below, and choose three of them. On a separate piece of paper, make three copies of the word web. In each, write the name of the movie or actor in the larger oval and adjectives in the smaller circles. You can refer to the adjectives you used in Activities 3 and 4, as well as any other adjectives you can think of. Then in the box below the ovals, write at least two sentences about each movie or actor. Be prepared to share your answers with the class.

Casablanca

Brad Pitt

Reese Witherspoon

Nicole Kidman

Harry Potter and the Goblet of Fire

Star Wars: Episode III

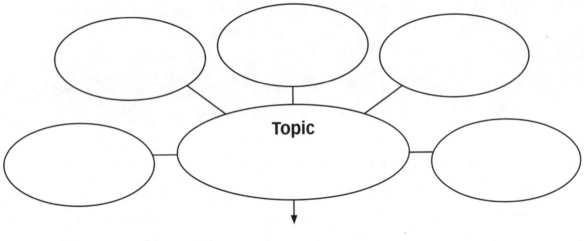

REPRODUCIBLE

Name _____   Date _____

Analyzing Movie Reviews

Directions: In small groups, use the questions below to analyze and critique at least three different movie reviews. Discuss the reviews with your group and take notes below. Be prepared to report back to the class on the reviews your group looked at.

1. Does the title of the review catch your attention? Why or why not?

2. Does the review identify the movie genre?

3. Does the review make use of interesting and appropriate adjectives?

4. Does the review identify the central actors in the movie and rate their performances?

5. Does the review give a brief summary of the story elements without spoiling the ending?

6. Does the review give the movie an overall rating?

7. Which of the movie reviews does the group like best and least? Be prepared to explain your reasons to the class.

Notes:

Review 1: _____

_____

_____

_____

_____

Review 2: _____

_____

_____

_____

_____

Review 3: _____

_____

_____

_____

_____

BLM 18

Name _____ Date _____

Using a Vocabulary Chart

Directions: Work in pairs or small groups. Look at all of the non-underlined words in the ten sentences from Activity 5. Write the words in the correct columns below. The first example is done for you. Be prepared to share your answers with the class.

Nouns	Verbs	Adjectives	Other
	is		

Name _____ Date _____

Using Transition Words and Phrases

Directions: Use the following transition words and phrases to rewrite and better unify the paragraph below: *however, in fact, in addition, also,* and *so . . . that.* When you are finished, exchange paragraphs with another student. Read your partner's work and make comments and suggestions.

    Last year was a great year for me at work. I think it might have been my best year ever. The accounts I was managing were successful. I got a promotion. I got a significant raise in salary. I got a bigger office. Not everything went perfectly for me. Some of my colleagues were jealous of my success. They became less friendly.

_____

_____

_____

_____

_____

_____

_____

_____

_____

Name _____ Date _____

Word Families

Directions: Work in pairs or small groups. Look at the words below from previous chapters. For each word, write as many words in the same word family as possible. Then write a sentence for each word in that family. Be prepared to identify the different parts of speech and the meanings of the words. The first example is done for you.

garden (noun), *gardener* (noun), *garden* (verb), *gardening* (gerund)

Fatima has a beautiful *garden*.

The wealthy family that lives down the street has two *gardeners*.

I like to *garden* in my free time.

Gardening can be a relaxing way to spend an afternoon.

interview _____

_____

_____

enjoy _____

_____

_____

social _____

_____

_____

explore _____

_____

_____

dance _____

_____

_____

entertain _____

_____

_____

BLM 21

Name _____   Date _____

The Ancient Olympic Games

Directions: Read the following information about the ancient Olympic Games, then write at least five sentences comparing the ancient Games with the modern Olympics. You can also use any information you gathered in your research for Activity 5. Use *both*, *but*, *however*, and the comparative forms of adjectives and adverbs. An example is done for you. Be prepared to share your sentences with the class.

The ancient Olympics had only ten events.

Only free men, no women, could compete in the games.

Only men who spoke Greek could compete in the games.

Any woman caught watching the Olympic Games would be killed.

The games were always held at Olympia.

Winning athletes at the games were treated as heroes.

A victor at the games received a crown made from olive leaves and was entitled to have a statue of himself set up at Olympia.

All Olympic judges were Eleans. Elis was the local region that included Olympia.

Winter Olympics were never held in Ancient Greece.

   Ancient Olympians competed nude; however, modern Olympians wear different types of

uniform depending on the sport.

_____

_____

_____

_____

_____

_____

_____

_____

_____

_____

_____

_____

BLM #3 Answer Key

1. She needs to save money, so she is working a part-time job. 2. He wants to watch the movie, but he doesn't have any time. 3. Fouad likes classical music. He also likes rock music. Also possible: Fouad likes classical music and rock music. 4. Karen likes tomatoes and carrots. 5. Yoshi doesn't have a notebook, so he needs to buy one. 6. Catherine is married and has two children. 7. Ali plays football on the weekend. He also does homework on the weekend. Or Ali plays football and does his homework on the weekend. 8. Tim has the CD, but he can't find it. 9. I'm not feeling well, so I need to see the doctor. 10. He really likes school and learning about the world.

BLM #12 Answer Key

When I was ten years old, my family went on vacation to Hawaii. **As soon as/When** we arrived, the Hawaiian girls put tropical flowers around our necks. **Then** we took a taxi to our hotel. **While** our parents were checking into the hotel, my sister and I went outside to see the ocean. Our hotel was right on the beach. **Then** we went to our rooms and put on our bathing suits. For seven days we swam in the ocean, ate delicious food, and did lots of fun activities. **When** we got home, we had so many great pictures to look at. It was our best vacation ever.

BLM #13 Answer Key

The Ugly Duckling, by Hans Christian Andersen

BLM #14 Answer Key

traditional (adjective) + *-ly* = traditionally (adverb)

thank (verb) + *-ful* = thankful (adjective)

mine (noun/verb) + *-er* = miner (noun)

selfish (adjective) + *-ly* = selfishly (adverb)

immediate (adjective) + *-ly* = immediately (adverb)

power (noun/verb) + *-ful* = powerful (adjective)

kind (adjective/noun) + *-ly* = kindly (adverb)

respect (noun/verb) + *-ful* = respectful (adjective)

farm (noun/verb) + *-er* = farmer (noun)

eventual (adjective) + *-ly* = eventually (adverb)

inform (verb) + *-al* = informal (adjective)

excite (verb) + *-ment* = excitement (noun)

BLM #16 Answer Key

Casablanca
Casablanca *is an exciting, romantic drama set in North Africa.*

Brad Pitt
Brad Pitt is a handsome actor who has been in many interesting films.

Reese Witherspoon
Reese Witherspoon is an Academy Award-winning actress. She is famous for her roles in the movies Walk the Line, Election, *and* Legally Blonde.

Nicole Kidman
Nicole Kidman is a gorgeous, talented actress who is also very funny.

Harry Potter and the Goblet of Fire
Harry Potter and the Goblet of Fire *is a terrifying, suspenseful movie. Harry has to pass difficult and frightening tests.*

Star Wars: Episode III
Star Wars: Episode III *has a great plot and wonderful special effects. The story is exciting and the acting is excellent.*

BLM #18 Answer Key

Nouns: hobby, Marcos, Blanca, she, time, Derek, family, trip, Phichai, Kim, mountains, Katie, she, lessons, five, Victor, things, year, Sam, Peter, he, time

Verbs: is, attended, had, took, has . . . been, has been . . . , was, has . . . , had, had

Adjectives: favorite, interested, many, this, many, no

Other: Aziza's, to, and, a, always, very, in, the, since, a, so, that, almost

BLM #19 Answer Key

Last year was a great year for me at work. <u>In fact</u>, I think it might have been my best year ever. The accounts I was managing were <u>so</u> successful <u>that</u> I got a promotion. <u>In addition</u>, I got a significant raise in salary. I <u>also</u> got a bigger office. <u>However</u>, not everything went perfectly for me. Some of my colleagues were <u>so</u> jealous of my success <u>that</u> they became less friendly.

BLM #20 Answer Key

interview (noun), *interview* (verb), *interviewer* (noun), *interviewing* (gerund)

enjoy (verb), *enjoyment* (noun), *enjoyable* (adjective), enjoying (gerund)

social (adjective), *socialize* (verb), *social* (noun), *sociable* (adjective), *socialite* (noun), socializing (gerund), socially (adverb)

explore (verb), *explorer* (noun), *exploration* (noun), exploratory (adjective), exploring (gerund)

dance (noun), *dance* (verb), *dancer* (noun), *dancing* (gerund)

entertain (verb), *entertainment* (noun), *entertainer* (noun), *entertaining* (adjective), entertaining (gerund)

Interactions 1 Writing Chapter 1 Test
Academic Life Around the World

Section I New Words/Expressions Match each word with its definition. Write the matching letter in the correct space. **(5 points each)**

_____	**1.** article	**a.**	true information
_____	**2.** classmates	**b.**	an idea for the future
_____	**3.** fact	**c.**	a collection of articles around one topic
_____	**4.** interview	**d.**	a story in a newspaper or magazine
_____	**5.** journal	**e.**	a newspaper, often with exaggerated or less serious news
_____	**6.** member	**f.**	a personal belief
_____	**7.** newsletter	**g.**	a person who belongs to a group
_____	**8.** opinion	**h.**	personal writings; a diary
_____	**9.** plan	**i.**	a series of questions and answers
_____	**10.** tabloid	**j.**	students in the same class

Section II Strategy Choose the letter of the best answer. **(5 points each)**

1. Which of these sentences is correct?
- Ⓐ Omar is also in my English class.
- Ⓑ Omar also is in my English class.
- Ⓒ Omar is in also my English class.

2. Which of these sentences is correct?
- Ⓐ Vanya thinks also the class is excellent.
- Ⓑ Vanya thinks the also class is excellent.
- Ⓒ Vanya also thinks the class is excellent.

3. Which sentence correctly introduces a result?
- Ⓐ His company does business in the United States, if he needs to learn English.
- Ⓑ His company does business in the United States, but he needs to learn English.
- Ⓒ His company does business in the United States, so he needs to learn English.

4. Which sentence correctly makes a contrast?

    Ⓐ Reiko can speak English well, but she needs to improve her writing skills.

    Ⓑ Reiko can speak English well, so she needs to improve her writing skills.

    Ⓒ Reiko can speak English well, and she needs to improve her writing skills.

5. Which sentence sounds the most natural?

    Ⓐ Mina is studying history and is studying art.

    Ⓑ Mina is studying history and studies art.

    Ⓒ Mina is studying history and art.

Section III Writing/Editing Skills Number the sentences in the most logical order from beginning to end. **(5 points each)**

_____ Some classes are good and others are not.

_____ There are many different English classes at our school.

_____ Good English classes have good teachers.

_____ The teachers know how to make the class interesting.

_____ The good classes all have one thing in common.

Interactions 1 Writing Chapter 2 Test
Experiencing Nature

Section I New Words/Expressions Decide if each word is a noun, adjective, or verb. Choose the letter of the best answer. **(5 points each)**

1. *nature*
- A noun
- B adjective
- C verb

2. *frightening*
- A noun
- B adjective
- C verb

3. *dark*
- A noun
- B adjective
- C verb

4. *background*
- A noun
- B adjective
- C verb

5. *describe*
- A noun
- B adjective
- C verb

6. *description*
- A noun
- B adjective
- C verb

7. *scene*
- A noun
- B adjective
- C verb

8. *artist*
- A noun
- B adjective
- C verb

9. *kill*
- A noun
- B adjective
- C verb

10. *dangerous*
- A noun
- B adjective
- C verb

Section II Strategy Choose the letter of the best answer. **(5 points each)**

1. Which sentence is correct?
- A The people in the painting are seated to the table.
- B The people in the painting are seated at a table.
- C The people in the painting are seated in the table.

2. Which sentence is **not** correct?
- A In the middle of the mural is a tree.
- B At the middle of the mural is a tree.
- C In the center of the mural is a tree.

3. Which sentence is correct?
- A The shark it is huge and frightening.
- B The shark is huge and frightening.
- C The shark huge and frightening is.

4. Which verb is not spelled correctly?
- (A) moves
- (B) moving
- (C) moveing

5. Which verb is not spelled correctly?
- (A) geting
- (B) untying
- (C) happening

Section III Writing/Editing Skills Number the sentences in the most logical order from beginning to end. **(5 points each)**

_____ Perhaps the man and woman are married, and the child is their baby.

_____ *The Boating Party* is a painting by Mary Cassatt.

_____ A woman and her child are seated in the front.

_____ It shows three people in a boat on a sunny day.

_____ The third person seems to be a man.

Interactions 1 Writing Chapter 3 Test
Living to Eat or Eating to Live?

Section I New Words/Expressions Match each word with its definition. Write the matching letter in the correct space. **(5 points each)**

_____ **1.** celebrate   **a.** a set of directions for making food

_____ **2.** dish   **b.** common, everyday

_____ **3.** ethnic   **c.** to make

_____ **4.** feast   **d.** to do something special for a special reason

_____ **5.** holiday   **e.** liked by many people

_____ **6.** popular   **f.** an ingredient that adds flavor

_____ **7.** prepare   **g.** a day of celebration

_____ **8.** recipe   **h.** a huge meal

_____ **9.** spice   **i.** prepared food

_____ **10.** typical   **j.** belonging to a particular culture

Section II Strategy Complete the following sentences. Choose the letter of the best answer. **(5 points each)**

1. A complete sentence must have a _____.
- Ⓐ fact and an opinion
- Ⓑ main idea and a detail
- Ⓒ subject and a verb

2. The words *a, an,* and *one* come before _____.
- Ⓐ count nouns
- Ⓑ noncount nouns
- Ⓒ pronouns

3. Noncount nouns such as *butter* and *rice* have no _____.
- Ⓐ plural forms
- Ⓑ regular forms
- Ⓒ simple forms

4. The phrase *such as* is used to introduce _____.

   (A) people

   (B) ideas

   (C) examples

5. An appositive must be separated from the rest of the sentence by _____.

   (A) commas

   (B) periods

   (C) parentheses

Section III Writing/Editing Skills Number the sentences in the most logical order from beginning to end. **(5 points each)**

_____ Typical dishes include turkey, yams, and cranberry sauce.

_____ On this day, American families usually sit down to a big meal.

_____ Thanksgiving is a traditional holiday.

_____ It falls on the third Thursday of November.

_____ Thanksgiving is my favorite holiday because I love to eat and be with my family.

Name _____ Date _____ Score _____

Interactions 1 Writing Chapter 4 Test
In the Community

Section I New Words/Expressions Match each word with its definition. Write the matching letter in the correct space. **(5 points each)**

_____	**1.** community	**a.** a public space or shopping area
_____	**2.** concert	**b.** a large grocery store
_____	**3.** directions	**c.** the people living in a city or town
_____	**4.** highway	**d.** instructions for finding a place
_____	**5.** landmark	**e.** a hall where films or plays are shown
_____	**6.** mall	**f.** a musical event
_____	**7.** movie	**g.** a major road for speedy travel
_____	**8.** salutation	**h.** an important building or place
_____	**9.** supermarket	**i.** a film
_____	**10.** theater	**j.** the greeting in a letter

Section II Strategy Choose the letter of the best answer. **(5 points each)**

1. Which sentence is correct?
- Ⓐ I am going to the movies every Friday.
- Ⓑ I go sometimes to the movies every Friday.
- Ⓒ I go to the movies every Friday.

2. Which sentence is **not** correct?
- Ⓐ The record store is at the mall.
- Ⓑ The record store is in the mall.
- Ⓒ The record store is on the mall.

3. Which sentence is correct?
- Ⓐ Take Highway 6 for Exit 14.
- Ⓑ Take Highway 6 in Exit 14.
- Ⓒ Take Highway 6 to Exit 14.

4. Which sentence is **not** correct?

   (A) There are many things to see in Washington.

   (B) There are an excellent museum in the city.

   (C) There is a monument in the park.

5. Which sentence is correct?

   (A) It is raining.

   (B) There is raining.

   (C) There rains.

Section III Writing/Editing Skills Number the sentences in the most logical order from beginning to end. **(5 points each)**

_____ There is an old section of San Juan and a new section.

_____ San Juan is the capital of Puerto Rico.

_____ I live in the old part of town.

_____ It is made entirely of stone and is very beautiful.

_____ There is a military fort in my neighborhood.

Interactions 1 Writing Chapter 5 Test
Home

Section I New Words/Expressions Match each word with its opposite. Write the matching letter in the correct space. **(5 points each)**

_____ **1.** baby   **a.** boring

_____ **2.** beginning   **b.** youngest

_____ **3.** was born   **c.** unusual

_____ **4.** exciting   **d.** ending

_____ **5.** happiest   **e.** friend

_____ **6.** oldest   **f.** teenager

_____ **7.** separation   **g.** saddest

_____ **8.** shy   **h.** self-confident

_____ **9.** stranger   **i.** died

_____ **10.** typical   **j.** reunion

Section II Strategy Choose the letter of the best answer. **(5 points each)**

1. Which sentence makes the most sense?
- (A) When I moved here I used to have many friends.
- (B) Before I moved here, I used to have many friends.
- (C) As soon as I moved here I used to have many friends.

2. Which sentence does **not** show time order?
- (A) I got a job as soon as I finished school.
- (B) I got a job after I finished school.
- (C) I got a job but I finished school.

3. Which sentence shows time order?
- (A) I changed jobs after I got married.
- (B) I changed jobs, and I got married.
- (C) I got married, but I didn't change jobs.

4. Which sentence gives a reason?

  (A) I cried quietly.

  (B) I cried because I had left my family.

  (C) I cried myself to sleep.

5. Which of the following is not a complete sentence?

  (A) As soon as I could.

  (B) I moved.

  (C) I was ten.

Section III Writing/Editing Skills Number the sentences in the most logical order from beginning to end. **(5 points each)**

_____ The separation was difficult, but I think it was good for us.

_____ We went to school together until the end of high school.

_____ I have a twin brother.

_____ I was born in 1979.

_____ When we graduated, we went to different colleges.

Interactions 1 Writing Chapter 6 Test
Cultures of the World

Section I New Words/Expressions Match each word with its definition. Write the matching letter in the correct space. **5 points each)**

_____   **1.** beef

a. likes to give

_____   **2.** bushel

b. a kind of meat

_____   **3.** castle

c. the lesson of a story

_____   **4.** culture

d. the home of a king or queen

_____   **5.** folktale

e. the traditions of a group of people

_____   **6.** generous

f. a traditional story

_____   **7.** hut

g. a large basket for vegetables

_____   **8.** jealous

h. envious

_____   **9.** miner

i. a person who digs for coal

_____   **10.** moral

j. a small house

Section II Strategy Complete the following sentences. Choose the letter of the best answer. **(5 points each)**

1. The words *before* and *after* are _____.
- Ⓐ time words
- Ⓑ articles
- Ⓒ clauses

2. The word *while* can be used to describe _____.
- Ⓐ one action that happened after another
- Ⓑ two actions separated by time
- Ⓒ two actions in progress at the same time

3. The phrase *as soon as* is used to show _____.
- Ⓐ that one action happened immediately after another
- Ⓑ two actions that are dependent on each other
- Ⓒ the reason for an action

4. The word *then* shows _____.
- (A) time order
- (B) reason
- (C) contrast

5. The first word of a quote always stars with a _____.
- (A) capital letter
- (B) preposition
- (C) vowel

Section III Writing/Editing Skills Read this text and then answer the following questions. **(5 points each)**

Phoenix Gives a Lesson

A Traditional Story from China

The phoenix is a very wise bird. In ancient times, other birds used to ask Phoenix for advice. One day all the birds went to see him at once. They wanted to know how to build a nest.

The phoenix began his instructions by saying, "To learn what I have to teach, you must listen carefully." The hen immediately fell asleep. The phoenix continued, "If you want to make a good nest, first you have to get three big branches and stack them on top of each other." The crow thought that was all he needed to know and flew away. Phoenix just shook his head and continued: "The best place to build a nest is under the eaves of a house. That way it will be safe from the wind and rain."

Swallow was the only one to hear every step. All the other birds had flown away or fallen asleep. Phoenix ended with this last piece of advice: "Mix mud with grass to make the nest strong." Swallow did exactly as Phoenix said.

Today, the hen does not know how to make a nest and lives on farms. The crow's nest is not very sturdy. The swallow makes his nest out of mud and grass and builds it under the eaves of people's homes. Only the swallow's nest is sturdy and safe from wind and rain.

1. This story is a _____.
- (A) folktale or fable
- (B) kind of puzzle
- (C) product of the author's imagination

2. How does the story get started?
- (A) The birds are all crowded together in the same nest.
- (B) Phoenix calls all the birds to come together.
- (C) All the birds ask Phoenix how to build a nest.

3. According to this story, what are the ingredients of a nest?
- (A) branches, mud, and grass
- (B) leaves and grass
- (C) wind and rain

4. How does the fable end?

    Ⓐ Each bird learns how to make its own kind of nest.

    Ⓑ Hen wakes up just in time to hear the last step.

    Ⓒ Swallow is the only bird who learns how to build a nest.

5. What seems to be the moral of this story?

    Ⓐ Learn to help yourself before you help others.

    Ⓑ You have to give in order to receive.

    Ⓒ Be patient and listen.

Interactions 1 Writing Chapter 7 Test
Health

Section I New Words/Expressions Match each word with a word that means the same or almost the same. Write the matching letter in the correct space. **(5 points each)**

_____ **1.** cure   **a.** physician

_____ **2.** doctor   **b.** customary

_____ **3.** effective   **c.** new

_____ **4.** herb   **d.** heal

_____ **5.** illness   **e.** useful

_____ **6.** medicine   **f.** sickness

_____ **7.** modern   **g.** drug

_____ **8.** pharmacy   **h.** drug store

_____ **9.** symptom   **i.** sign

_____ **10.** traditional   **j.** plant

Section II Strategy Choose the letter of the best answer. **(5 points each)**

1. Which sentence correctly uses the word *that*?
   - (A) People take aspirin that is a common medicine.
   - (B) Aspirin is a common medicine that is used for headaches.
   - (C) Aspirin that is a common medicine cures headaches.

2. Which sentence correctly uses the word *who*?
   - (A) Herbalists are healers who use plants.
   - (B) Herbs are plants who are able to cure some illnesses.
   - (C) Traditional doctors use plants who are herbs.

3. Which sentence correctly uses the phrase *in addition*?
   - (A) Some doctors use herbs in addition of tea and bark.
   - (B) Some doctors use herbs in addition to illness.
   - (C) Some doctors use herbs in addition to modern medicine.

4. Which sentence is correctly formed?

    (A) I drank herbal tea cures my sore throat.

    (B) I drank herbal tea to cure my sore throat.

    (C) I drank herbal tea curing my sore throat.

5. Which sentence is a run-on sentence?

    (A) You should eat well and get plenty of sleep in addition you should exercise.

    (B) To stay healthy, you need to eat well, get plenty of sleep, and exercise.

    (C) People need to eat well and get plenty of sleep to stay healthy.

Section III Writing/Editing Skills Number the sentences in the most logical order from beginning to end. **(5 points each)**

_____ For example, I know a woman who had cancer.

_____ Some people can cure themselves with traditional remedies.

_____ She drank an herbal tea every day for several months.

_____ After following the treatment for five months, the cancer was gone.

_____ In addition, she practiced yoga and meditation.

Interactions 1 Writing Chapter 8 Test
Entertainment and the Media

Section I New Words/Expressions Match each word with its opposite. Write the letter in the correct space. **(5 points each)**

_____ **1.** ambitious   **a.** quiet

_____ **2.** brilliant   **b.** boring

_____ **3.** courageous   **c.** kind

_____ **4.** egotistical   **d.** outgoing

_____ **5.** entertaining   **e.** ugly

_____ **6.** evil   **f.** lazy

_____ **7.** gorgeous   **g.** stupid

_____ **8.** innocent   **h.** fearful

_____ **9.** shy   **i.** experienced

_____ **10.** talkative   **j.** modest

Section II Strategy Complete the following sentences. Choose the letter of the best answer. **(5 points each)**

1. A good movie summary includes _____.
  Ⓐ interesting details
  Ⓑ the most important events
  Ⓒ bits of dialogue

2. Titles of films should be _____.
  Ⓐ italicized or underlined
  Ⓑ written in capital letters
  Ⓒ put in parentheses

3. Adjectives _____ characters and events.
  Ⓐ name
  Ⓑ describe
  Ⓒ identify

4. Appositives can be used to _____.

- Ⓐ combine sentences
- Ⓑ separate sentences
- Ⓒ fragment sentences

5. The historical present tense is used to describe events in the _____.

- Ⓐ past
- Ⓑ present
- Ⓒ future

Section III Writing/Editing Skills Number the sentences in their most logical order. **(5 points each)**

_____ It tells the story of Jack and Rose, two people who meet on a ship.

_____ *Titanic* is a tragic love story.

_____ Then the ship hits an iceberg and sinks.

_____ Sadly, Jack dies, but Rose survives.

_____ They fall in love at first sight.

Interactions 1 Writing Chapter 9 Test
Social Life

Section I New Words/Expressions Decide if each word is a noun, adjective, or verb. Write the word in the correct column below. **(5 points each)**

1. hobby

2. accomplish

3. responsible

4. enjoyment

5. juggler

6. fascinating

7. attend

8. rainy

9. recreation

10. busy

Noun	Adjective	Verb

Section II Strategy Choose the letter of the best answer. **(5 points each)**

1. Which of these sentences is correct?
- (A) Nina was happy so that she cried.
- (B) Nina was so happy that she cried.
- (C) Nina so happy was that she cried.

2. Which of these sentences has correct capitalization?

    (A) Abdul is attending Stanford university in California.

    (B) I've been studying Japanese since july.

    (C) Van will go to New York City College next year.

3. Which sentence is correct?

    (A) Michael is going to school and working at the same time.

    (B) Michael going to school and working at the same time.

    (C) Michael has been going to school and was working at the same time.

4. Which sentence is **not** correct?

    (A) Paige has known Kelly for about ten years.

    (B) Paige knew Kelly for about ten years.

    (C) Paige has been knowing Kelly for about ten years.

5. Which sentence is in the present perfect continuous tense?

    (A) Corey worked full time for three months.

    (B) Corey has worked full time for three months.

    (C) Corey has been working full time for three months.

Section III Writing/Editing Skills Number the sentences from most general to most specific.
(5 points each)

_____   She also works so that she can pay her tuition.

_____   Adrianne has had a very busy year.

_____   She has been going to school full time.

_____   In addition, she is getting married in June.

_____   Her fiancé is very understanding, because he's a student, too.

Interactions 1 Writing Chapter 10 Test

Sports

Section I New Words/Expressions Complete the following sentences. Choose the letter of the best answer. **(5 points each)**

1. Horseback riding is a(n) _____ sport.
- (A) team
- (B) individual
- (C) safe

2. You need to have at least two _____ to play tennis.
- (A) competitors
- (B) spectators
- (C) fans

3. There can be only one _____.
- (A) winner
- (B) win
- (C) winning

4. We were very disappointed because the _____ team won.
- (A) oppose
- (B) opposing
- (C) opponent

5. "I didn't see the end of the game. What was the final _____?"
- (A) point
- (B) goal
- (C) score

6. She won the gold medal at the Olympics. She is very _____.
- (A) crazy
- (B) talented
- (C) dangerous

7. I don't like team sports. I prefer _____ sports.
- (A) competitive
- (B) professional
- (C) individual

8. Our team _____ the challenger and are the champions!
- (A) defeated
- (B) lost
- (C) scored

9. If you don't like heights, _____ is not the sport for you.

- (A) in-line skating
- (B) rock climbing
- (C) ice skating

10. The _____ was delayed because of the rain.

- (A) competition
- (B) goal
- (C) point

Section II Strategy Circle the letter of the correct answer. (5 points each)

1. Which of these sentences is correct?

- (A) He is a gooder student than they are.
- (B) She is a worser student than he is.
- (C) He is a better student than I am.

2. Which of these sentences has correct punctuation?

- (A) Boxing is a violent sport but, I like it
- (B) Boxing is a violent sport; however, I like it.
- (C) Boxing is a violent sport. However I like it.

3. Which sentence is correct?

- (A) Both scuba diving and skydiving require a lot of equipment.
- (B) Skydiving and rock climbing require both a lot of experience.
- (C) Scuba diving and rock climbing are dangerous both.

4. Which sentence is **not** correct?

- (A) He can run more quickly than I can.
- (B) He is quick than I am.
- (C) He is quicker than I am.

5. Which sentence shows similarities?

- (A) He likes individual sports; however, she likes soccer.
- (B) I am fast, but she is faster.
- (C) Both players are energetic.

Section III Writing/Editing Skills Number the sentences in the most logical order from beginning to end. (5 points each)

_____ On the other hand, there are some similarities.

_____ The ancient Olympics were quite different from the modern games.

_____ All in all, I think I prefer our modern games.

_____ For example, there were only ten events, and only men were allowed to compete.

_____ For example, like today, winners at the games were treated as heroes.

Chapter 1 Test Answer Key

Section I

1. d 2. j 3. a 4. i 5. h 6. g 7. c 8. f 9. b 10. e

Section II

1. a 2. c 3. c 4. a 5. c

Section III

2 1 4 5 3

Chapter 2 Test Answer Key

Section I

1. a 2. b 3. b 4. a 5. c 6. a 7. a 8. a 9. c 10. b

Section II

1. b 2. b 3. b 4. c 5. a

Section III

1. 5 2. 1 3. 3 4. 2 5. 4

Chapter 3 Test Answer Key

Section I

1. d 2. i 3. j 4. h 5. g 6. e 7. c 8. a 9. f 10. b

Section II

1. c 2. a 3. a 4. c 5. a

Section III

4 3 1 2 5

Chapter 4 Test Answer Key

Section I

1. c 2. f 3. d 4. g 5. h 6. a 7. i
8. j 9. b 10. e

Section II

1. c 2. c 3. c 4. b 5. a

Section III

2 1 3 5 4

Chapter 5 Test Answer Key

Section I

1. f 2. d 3. i 4. a 5. g 6. b 7. j 8. h 9. e 10. c

Section II

1. b 2. c 3. a 4. b 5. a

Section III

5 3 2 1 4

Chapter 6 Test Answer Key

Section I

1. b 2. g 3. d 4. e 5. f 6. a 7. j 8. h 9. i 10. c

Section II

1. a 2. c 3. a 4. a 5. a

Section III

1. a 2. c 3. a 4. c 5. c

Chapter 7 Test Answer Key

Section I

1. d 2. a 3. e 4. j 5. f 6. g 7. c 8. h 9. i 10. b

Section II

1. b 2. a 3. c 4. b 5. a

Section III

2 1 3 5 4

Chapter 8 Test Answer Key

Section I

1. f 2. g 3. h 4. j 5. c 6. b 7. e 8. i 9. d 10. a

Section II

1. b 2. a 3. b 4. a 5. a

Section III

2 1 4 5 3

Chapter 9 Test Answer Key

Section I

Noun	Adjective	Verb
hobby	responsible	accomplish
enjoyment	fascinating	attend
juggler	rainy	
recreation	busy	

Section II

1. b 2. c 3. a 4. c 5. c

Section III

3 1 2 4 5

Chapter 10 Test Answer Key

Section I

1. b 2. a 3. a 4. b 5. c 6. b 7. c 8. a 9. b 10. a

Section II

1. c 2. b 3. a 4. b 5. c

Section III

3 1 5 2 4

Writing Placement Test

Section I Sentence Completion Choose the letter of the best word, words, or phrase to complete each sentence. **(1 point each)**

Example: I want the pretty necklace _____.
- Ⓐ that is on sale
- Ⓑ who is on sale
- Ⓒ what is on sale
- Ⓓ where it is on sale

1. The restaurant has excellent food, _____.
   - Ⓐ so I never eat there
   - Ⓑ so I always eat there
   - Ⓒ I never eat there
   - Ⓓ I always eat there

2. I want to go to Mexico, _____.
   - Ⓐ but I have a lot of money
   - Ⓑ but I don't speak Spanish fluently
   - Ⓒ but I speak Spanish fluently
   - Ⓓ I speak Spanish fluently

3. There's a movie theater _____ the left hand side of the street.
   - Ⓐ at
   - Ⓑ in
   - Ⓒ on
   - Ⓓ off

4. Louise screamed, _____
   - Ⓐ There's a fire upstairs!
   - Ⓑ "There's a fire upstairs!"
   - Ⓒ "That there is a fire upstairs!"
   - Ⓓ There's "a fire upstairs!"

5. She ate lunch _____.
   - Ⓐ as soon as she finished writing the report
   - Ⓑ when the report ends
   - Ⓒ while the report ends
   - Ⓓ soon as the meeting ended

6. The teacher _____ tells jokes in class is very popular.
   - Ⓐ what
   - Ⓑ which
   - Ⓒ who
   - Ⓓ there

7. Another easy-to-prepare dish is quiche, _____.
   - (A) what is wonderful for lunch
   - (B) is brunch
   - (C) is wonderful for brunch
   - (D) which is wonderful for brunch

8. _____ I broke my leg, I have had a great deal of difficulty getting around.
   - (A) When
   - (B) While
   - (C) Since
   - (D) As soon as

9. She doesn't eat sugary foods _____.
   - (A) because she wants to gain weight
   - (B) because she wants to lose weight
   - (C) but she wants to lose weight
   - (D) when she wants to gain weight

10. I can't go out for dinner tonight _____.
    - (A) because storms often come
    - (B) because a storm is coming
    - (C) because I love to go out for dinner
    - (D) because there will be a storm tomorrow at dinner time

11. It is important to exercise regularly _____ you stay in good shape.
    - (A) so that
    - (B) because
    - (C) unless
    - (D) as a result

12. I saw an apartment that I loved; _____ the rent was too high.
    - (A) so,
    - (B) however,
    - (C) therefore,
    - (D) in addition,

13. "Where did you park the car?" Stan asked.
    "It's _____ the fire hydrant," Marta replied.
    - (A) on top of
    - (B) below
    - (C) next to
    - (D) in

14. _____ my sister, I am a stay-at-home mom.
    - (A) Similar
    - (B) Similarly
    - (C) Different of
    - (D) Unlike

15. The man was convicted for _____.
- (A) stealing a car
- (B) because he stole
- (C) to steal
- (D) stolen car

Section II Organization Read the following sentences. Circle the letter of the sentence that best follows the sentence given. **(2 points each)**

Example: This morning we ate the most wonderful blueberry waffles for breakfast.
- (A) I like meat and potatoes.
- (B) I eat blueberries every night.
- (C) My husband made some delicious coffee to go with the waffles.
- (D) I don't like coffee.

1. Children often have trouble getting up in the morning to go to school.
- (A) For example, children love to get up in the morning.
- (B) This is probably because many kids stay up late.
- (C) Once children get to school, they can take naps.
- (D) Children always like going to school and try to be punctual.

2. The Mexican government is trying to decrease pollution in Mexico City.
- (A) They will try a number of different approaches to increase this problem.
- (B) I don't worry about pollution very much.
- (C) Some people who live outside of the city think that pollution is not a problem.
- (D) They have written many new laws to limit driving and industrial pollution.

3. It is very simple to make microwave popcorn.
- (A) Popcorn always gets stuck between my teeth.
- (B) I don't know how much popcorn costs.
- (C) I buy popcorn when I go to the movies.
- (D) All you have to do is put a bag in the microwave and press a button.

4. I firmly believe that children under the age of 21 should not be allowed to smoke.
- (A) I think that smoking is something that young people enjoy doing.
- (B) I don't have any strong feelings about teenage smoking.
- (C) My family was very poor and could not afford to buy cigarettes for my mother.
- (D) Teenagers don't always understand the dangers of smoking.

5. Thank you so much for the gorgeous necklace.
- (A) You should have bought something that was a little more expensive.
- (B) Necklaces always look better on women who are much younger than I am.
- (C) I have worn it several times and always receive compliments.
- (D) Next time can we please go shopping for necklaces together?

6. I love to watch movies.
- (A) Last weekend, I saw three films.
- (B) My brother works in Hollywood.
- (C) Last weekend, my DVD player broke.
- (D) Maybe we can go to see a play this weekend.

7. Echinacea is an herbal remedy for the common cold.

   (A) It was cold at the doctor's office this morning.

   (B) I need to buy more Vitamin C.

   (C) People who take it say that Vitamin C tastes good.

   (D) People who take it say that it decreases the length of their illness.

8. There are benefits of growing up in a large family.

   (A) Families that eat together, laugh together.

   (B) For example, I have three brothers and four sisters.

   (C) For example, there are too many people to cook for.

   (D) For example, my older sister gives me a lot of her clothes.

9. People over the age of 100 should not be allowed to drive.

   (A) My grandmother is 105.

   (B) Last year, the oldest woman in the world died at 111.

   (C) As people get older, their vision gets worse.

   (D) Some people enjoy their lives more after the age of eighty.

10. Thailand is an informal country.

    (A) Suits are worn for all occasions.

    (B) Suits are worn for only business and other important occasions.

    (C) It is important to dress well.

    (D) It is important to stay dry in the monsoons.

Section III Sentence Ordering Read the following sentences. Then number them from 1–5, as you would arrange them in a paragraph. **(5 points each)**

Example Writing:

____4____ Once you have a completed a draft, revise for content, as some of the ideas may not be in a logical order.

____2____ To begin, spend time brainstorming, or thinking of ideas.

____5____ Finally, edit for grammatical errors.

____1____ Writing is a process.

____3____ Then, write a first draft.

1. World Cup Soccer

_____ Italy won the final match.

_____ World Cup Soccer is an international sporting event.

_____ In 2006, the World Cup Finals were hosted by Germany.

_____ Thirty-two teams went to Germany to compete against each other for a month.

_____ Teams from all over the world compete to play in the World Cup Finals, which are held in a different location every four years.

2. San Francisco

_____ Most people don't know that the city was built on 43 hills.

_____ The steepest hill is in the Russian Hill neighborhood of the city.

_____ San Francisco is a city in Northern California.

_____ This is also the part of San Francisco where tourists go to see the famous "Crooked Street."

_____ It is considered one of the most beautiful cities in North America.

3. Floods

_____ Flash floods can be more destructive than most other types of natural disasters.

_____ Every year, they cause billions of dollars in damage.

_____ They happen when there has been a heavy rainstorm that causes a river to quickly swell and spill over, often flooding roads and developed land.

_____ If the water can not be cleaned up right away, it causes more damage.

_____ Once roads are flooded, it is very difficult to get rescue and clean-up equipment to the people who need them.

4. Only Children

_____ Only children often have higher self-esteem than other people.

_____ Some people think all this positive attention can make only children selfish and anti-social.

_____ But this is not true.

_____ In fact, the positive attention allows only children to be outgoing and generous.

_____ Because they receive more attention from their parents then children with siblings, they have an easier time keeping a positive view of themselves.

Part IV Your teacher will tell you if you should write a paragraph or an essay.

Write a Paragraph

Choose one of the following topics listed below, and write a paragraph about it. Feel free to make some notes on a separate sheet of paper before you start writing. The paragraph is worth up to 45 points.

1. Think of the different foods that you like to eat when you are at home. Compare and contrast two of your favorite foods.

2. Think about the different places people go on vacation. Write about a place you would like to go for a vacation. What are the advantages of that location? What makes it better than other places?

3. Think about your favorite time of day and why you like it best. Use details to describe your favorite time of day and why it's your favorite.

Write an Essay

Choose one of the topics listed below and write an essay about it. The essay is worth up to 45 points.

1. Think about the different academic subjects you have studied. Compare and contrast one that you liked and one that you didn't like.

2. Without proper role models, it is impossible to succeed. What is your view on this subject? Do you agree or disagree with this statement? Please provide examples to support your opinion.

3. Some people believe that walking, riding a bike, or taking the subway are better modes of transportation than driving a car. What are the advantages and disadvantages of these different modes of transportation? Please write an argument in favor of one or more modes of transportation.

Writing Placement Test Note to Teachers:

All students will do Parts 1–3 of the Writing Placement Test. When you get to Part 4, it is your choice whether students write the paragraph or the essay, depending on their level. Either way, Part 4 is worth up to 45 points.

Placement Test Answer Key and Scoring Rubrics

Section I Each question is worth 1 point, for a total of 15 points for this section.

Example: a

1. b 2. b 3. c 4. b 5. a 6. c 7. d 8. c 9. b 10. b 11. a
12. b 13. c 14. d 15. a

Section II Each question is worth 2 points, for a total of 20 points for this section.

Example: c

1. b 2. d 3. d 4. d 5. c 6. a 7. d 8. d 9. c 10. b

Section III Each question is worth 5 points, for a total of 20 points for this section.

Example: 4 2 5 1 3

1. 5 1 3 4 2

2. 3 4 1 5 2

3. 1 2 3 5 4

4. 1 3 4 5 2

Section IV Writing Test Rubric

Students will write either the paragraph or the essay. Each is worth up to 45 points.

Use the rubric below to score Part 4. The rubric contains five categories: content, organization, vocabulary, grammar, and spelling and mechanics. For each category, decide if the writing is best described by *Excellent*, *Adequate*, or *Developing*. Then score that category based on the points listed in the rubric.

Writing Rubric

Score	Description
31–45 points **Excellent**	**Content:** Writing presents enough information so that the reader has a clear idea of the topic. The writing is interesting and well-developed. **Organization:** Paragraph(s) have topic sentence(s). Ideas move smoothly from general to specific or in another clear, logical order. Related details are grouped together. **Vocabulary:** Words are specific, varied, and used correctly throughout. **Grammar:** Verb tenses are used correctly. Overall, there are few grammar mistakes, and the meaning of the sentences is clear. **Spelling and Mechanics:** Most words are spelled correctly and punctuation is used correctly.

16–30 points Adequate	**Content:** Writing presents information about the topic, but the reader is left with questions. **Organization:** Paragraph(s) is/are focused, but some related details are not grouped together or may not connect to the topic. Ideas may not move from general to specific or in any clear and logical order. **Vocabulary:** Vocabulary is specific and varied, but some words may be used incorrectly. **Grammar:** Verb tenses are used correctly and the meaning of the sentences is clear, but there are some grammar mistakes. **Spelling and Mechanics:** Writing includes some spelling and/or punctuation mistakes.
0–15 points Developing	**Content:** Writing does not present enough information about the topic and contains too many unrelated ideas. **Organization:** Topic sentence(s) are not used. Order of ideas is confusing. **Vocabulary:** Vocabulary is limited or repetitive, and/or there are too many mistakes to understand the ideas. **Grammar:** There are many grammar problems, including verb mistakes, which make the ideas difficult to follow. **Spelling and Mechanics:** Writing includes many distracting spelling and/or punctuation mistakes.

SCORING FOR INTERACTIONS/MOSAIC WRITING PLACEMENT TEST	
Score	**Placement**
0–27	Interactions Access
28–46	Interactions 1
47–65	Interactions 2
66–84	Mosaic 1
85–100	Mosaic 2

This is a rough guide. Teachers should use their judgment in placing students and selecting texts.